THE DINGLE, IVERAGH & BEARA PENINSULAS

Adrian Hendroff a qualified Mountain Leader, is a photographer and writer on Ireland's mountains. He is one of the few to have ascended all 268 of Ireland's summits over 600m. His articles have featured in magazines such as *TGO, Walking World Ireland* and *Irish Mountain Log*. He has also walked in the mountain ranges of Scotland, Wales, England, Romania, Iceland, and the Alps and Dolomites, but he thinks of the Irish mountains as home. His previous book, *From High Places: A Journey Through Ireland's Great Mountains*, was published in 2010. He is also a member of the Outdoor Writers and Photographers Guild, www.owpg. org.uk.

www.adrianhendroff.com

Acknowledgements

There are several people whose encouragement, participation and support were invaluable during the making of this guidebook, and to whom I owe a huge debt of gratitude. In particular, I would like to thank my wife, Una, for her love, patience and the proof-reading. Thanks also to The Collins Press for their expertise, patience and ongoing support. For their kind hospitality and putting up with my early starts I should thank: Brendan and Geraldine Ceallaigh, Dave and Maria Williams, Denise Kane, Maureen and John Fleming. For assistance with Irish–English translations and place-name meanings, thanks to: Aonghus Ó hAlmhain and also Pádraig Ó Dálaigh and Sean McGlinchey of The Placenames Branch. Thanks to my friends Barry Speight, Charles O'Byrne, John Fitzgerald, John Noble and Richie Casey. Thanks for various reasons to Anne Barlow, Beara Tourism, Dingle Peninsula Tourism, Gerry Christie, Helen Lawless of Mountaineering Ireland, John Cronin, Julian English, Maurice Breen and Sarah Seery of Kerry Outdoor Sports. Finally, to the people I've met or who have accompanied me on the trail: Blathnaid, Declan, Donal, Hilde, John, Mary, Miah, Micheal, Mossie, Paddy, Patrick, Peter, Piotr, Sean, Susan and Tanya. For those I have forgotten to mention, please accept my apology in advance, as this is merely an oversight.

Edition notes

Ascent routes for Eagle Mountain (Walk 1) and the Cloon Horseshoe (Walk 15) have been revised due to access reasons. A minor revision to parking for The Coomloughra Horseshoe (Walk 18) has also been added.

The view northeast down into the Baurearagh valley from the col south eastwards of the Caha plateau.

THE DINGLE, IVERAGH & BEARA PENINSULAS

A Walking Guide

Adrian Hendroff

The Collins Press

For Una and grandpa,
and in special memory of Joss

FIRST PUBLISHED IN 2011 BY
The Collins Press
West Link Park
Doughcloyne
Wilton
Cork

Reprinted 2012, 2014

British Library Cataloguing in Publication Data
Hendroff, Adrian.
The Dingle, Iveragh & Beara Peninsulas : a walking guide.
1. Walking–Ireland–Dingle Peninsula–Guidebooks.
2. Walking–Ireland–Iveragh Peninsula–Guidebooks.
3. Walking–Ireland–Beara Peninsula–Guidebooks.
4. Dingle Peninsula (Ireland)–Guidebooks. 5. Iveragh
Peninsula (Ireland)–Guidebooks. 6. Beara Peninsula
(Ireland)–Guidebooks.
I. Title
796.5'1'09419-dc22

ISBN-13: 9781848891036

Design and typesetting by Fairways Design

Typeset in Avenir

Printed in Poland by Białostockie Zakłady Graficzne SA

Contents

Beara Peninsula

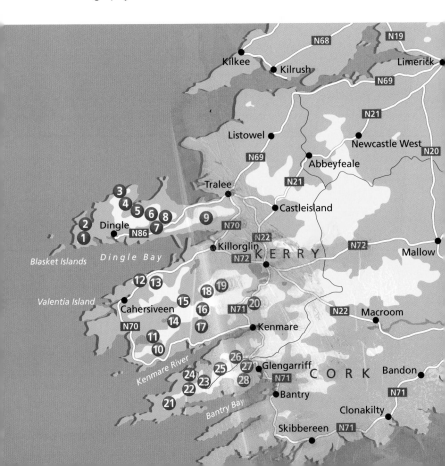

Introduction

And there I asked beneath a lonely cloud
Of strange delight, with one bird singing loud,
What change you'd wrought in graveyard, rock and sea,
This new wild paradise to wake for me . . .
Yet knew no more than knew those merry sins
Had built this stack of thigh-bones, jaws and shins.

— John Millington Synge ('In Kerry')

Synge calls it a 'wild paradise' and its mountains a 'stack of thigh-bones, jaws and shins'. I couldn't agree more, having enjoyed nearly over a decade of exploring the mountains in this irresistible corner of Ireland.

It is astonishing to think that during the Devonian Period, about 410 to 350 million years ago, this region was an arid, hot and low-lying alluvial plain. Sediments of substantial thickness were deposited by southward-flowing seasonal rivers. These sedimentary layers formed the distinctive reddish or purplish-coloured Old Red Sandstone rock that is common to this region today. Chaos followed. A mountain-building episode 340 to 280 million years ago resulted in tectonic forces compressing and thrusting up layers of rock in east–west folds. The mountains of Kerry and Cork were born during this Hercynian or Variscan orogeny.

The peaks of the Dingle, Iveragh and Beara Peninsulas were then of Alpine proportions. However, erosion, hard weathering and glaciations of the past 280 million years have gnawed away at these giant peaks, trimming them to their present size. The hard sandstone cores resisted erosion and their defiance formed today's sandstone rock ridges, slabs and ribs that make up most of the highlands of these peninsulas.

Ice then became the master sculptor from about 2 million years ago on more than one occasion. Monstrous tongues of ice pushed their way northwards and northwestwards across these peninsulas carving deep, steep-sided and lake-filled corries; forming hanging valleys; dragging large boulders and depositing moraine sediments along the valley floors.

We have much to thank this epoch of geological landscape-building for as we walk the rugged peaks, dramatic ridges, captivating valleys and glittering lakes of the Dingle, Iveragh and Beara Peninsulas in the present time.

My first mountain in this region was Slievanea (620m/2,034ft) in the Dingle Peninsula nearly a decade ago. My wife, Una, and I parked along the Conor Pass Road and scrambled up a rocky crest to its level, curved, summit area. There, I was struck by a myriad of shapes and colours that adorned the landscape: the silver-blue strings of glinting streams, dark-blue lakes, wide brownish-green valleys, russet-brown moorland, sepia mountains, the steel-blue sea and a cloud-filled sky. This view uplifted me in more ways than one.

I have returned to the pointed finger of Dingle countless times since, each time exploring a new mountain, valley, gully or lake. In between, I have also been drawn to visit the mountains on the plump knuckle of Iveragh to its south, and the little finger of Beara further still. There is a treasure chest of mountains and hundreds of walking options waiting to be discovered, each offering the chance to escape from an increasingly rushed and weary world.

There is too much to write about these peninsulas to pack into an introduction, so allow me to reveal its secrets in a collection of 28 carefully selected routes. Iveragh is broader, so I have decided to give it more walks than Dingle and Beara. The hillwalking routes are designed to cover the length of each peninsula (and if you look at maps they *are* long!) in a general west to east direction. In selecting the routes, I have tailored the majority of them to be different from previous guidebooks and I often also provide a range of options and extensions.

I hope that this guidebook will lead to many great mountain days of your own in this exhilarating corner of Ireland. For every one walk in this guidebook, I can think of another half dozen variations, so finishing all the routes is not the end of exploration!

The majority of these walking routes and mountains are quiet; for most of the time I have not encountered a soul. So revel in the freedom of the hills, and enjoy the peace and comfort it brings.

Happy walking!

Adrian Hendroff

Using This Book

Maps

The maps in this book are approximate representations of the routes only. For all routes in this guidebook, the use of detailed maps is imperative. All maps listed below are Ordnance Survey Ireland (OSi) Discovery Series 1:50 000 unless otherwise stated. Laminated versions are recommended for durability in wind and rain. Note that 1:50 000 OSi maps do not show cliffs, crags, boulder-fields or areas of scree. Also, forestry and tracks may also change from time to time, so it is useful to get the latest edition.

The following maps are required for this guidebook:
- **Dingle Peninsula:** OSi Sheet 70 and 71.
- **Iveragh Peninsula:** OSi Sheet 78 and 83.
- **Beara Peninsula:** OSi Sheet 84 and 85.

Note there are even more detailed maps of the MacGillycuddy's Reeks:
- *OSi MacGillycuddy's Reeks* 1:25 000
- Harvey *Superwalker MacGillycuddy's Reeks* 1:30 000 – this map shows tracks and cliffs in detail and a summit enlargement of Carrauntoohil at 1:15 000.

Grid References

Grid references (e.g. **Q 315**10 **007**37) provided in this book should help you plan a route and upload it to your GPS or to use your GPS to check a grid reference on the mountain. Set your GPS to use the Irish Grid (IG). Note that GPS units are precise to 5 digits, whereas a 3-digit precision will usually suffice using map and compass, and hence these are outlined in **bold**.

Walking Times

Walking times in this book are calculated based on individual speeds of 3 to 4km per hour. One minute has been added for every 10m of ascent, so for example if a height gain of 600m is the case, an hour would be added to the total walking time. A 6km walk with a total of 300m ascent will take 2 to 2½ hours.

In some routes, I have compensated for the seriousness of terrain, for example, the Beenkeragh arête in Walk 18 and the Big Gun ridge in Walk 19. In other cases, in a long walk back by road, for instance you may find yourself walking at 5 km per hour.

Note that the Walking Time stated in the routes of this guidebook does **not** include the additional time required for stops.

Metric and imperial units are given for road approaches (as some vehicles may be still using miles), total distance, total ascent and mountain heights. However, walking distances are given in metric to conform to OSi maps.

Walk Grades

Walks in this book are graded 1 to 5 based on *level of difficulty*, with 1 being the easiest and 5 the hardest.

Walk grades 1 and 2 should be comfortable to all beginner hillwalkers where little or easy navigation is required, and the overall length of the walk is short. The length of a grade 1 walk is the shortest, and a grade 2 slightly longer.

Walks graded 3 or higher should only be undertaken by hillwalkers who are competent in the use of map, compass and navigational skills. These walks also imply a half to a full day's outing in the hills, and some straightforward to moderate steep ground.

The previous recommendation applies for walks graded 4, but in addition factor complex terrain and moderate to difficult steep ground into the equation. Expect to be out for a full day in the hills.

The previous recommendation applies for walks graded 5, with the addition of difficult steep ground with some easy to medium scrambling.

Access

All land in the Republic of Ireland is owned privately or by the State, with no legal right of entry to the land. When you hear the term 'commonage' it implies that the private property is held in common by a number of joint owners.

Access to upland and mountain areas has traditionally been granted out of the goodwill, permission and discretion of the owners. It is normally good practice to strike up a friendly conversation with a farmer or landowner, and if there is any doubt about access, do ask them.

Note also that the provisions of the Occupiers Liability Act 1995 contain a definition that reduces the landowner's duty of care to hillwalkers. This act contains a category of 'recreational users' who, when they enter farmland, are responsible for their own safety. This has significantly reduced the possibility of successful legal claims against landowners by hillwalkers.

Mountain Safety

1. Get a detailed weather forecast. Useful sources of information are www.met.ie, www.irishweatheronline.ie and the mountain forecast on www.accuweather.com.

2. There is a temperature drop of 2–3 °C for every 300m of ascent. If it is a pleasant morning at sea level it could be cold on the summit of Carrauntoohil at 1,040m! The wind is also 2½ times stronger at 900m as it is at sea level. Wind velocities at a col are higher and wind effects can be strong on an exposed ridge.

3. Keep well away from cliff edges. Be cautious of wet or slippery rock and holes in the ground on vegetated slopes. Take your time traversing a boulder field, descending a scree slope and during scrambling.

4. Streams in flood are dangerous and water levels can rise quickly.

5. Ensure that you and your equipment are up to the task, and know the limitations of both. Winter conditions require specialised gear.

6. Be aware of daylight hours for the time of year. Most accidents happen during descent or near the end of the day. Carry enough emergency equipment (e.g. a survival shelter) should an injury occur and you need to stop moving.

7. It is recommended not to walk alone, except in areas where there are other people around. Leave word with someone responsible.

8. Do not leave any valuables in cars. Keep all things in the boot and out of sight to avoid unwanted attention.

9. Carry a fully charged mobile phone, but keep it well away from the compass as its needle is affected by metal.

10. In case of emergency call 999/112 and ask for 'Mountain Rescue'. Before dialling, it helps to be ready to give a grid location of your position.

Tip: I recommend the use of a plastic tube about 50cm long, slit into half along its length. This aids crossing barbed-wire fences and also prevents damage to them.

WALK 1: MOUNTAIN OF THE EAGLE

Mount Eagle (516m/1,693ft), or *Sliabh an Iolair* in Irish, rises above the spectacular coastal road around Slea Head and the beak-like projection of Dunmore Head on the western tip of the Dingle Peninsula. The hike up to its summit is a perfect introduction to hillwalking on the Dingle Peninsula. The smell of the sea air and the sight of lovely rolling hills is an intoxicating mix. The lower part of the walk takes in charming country lanes and Dunmore Head while the higher sections offer magnificent views of Dingle's Atlantic coastline.

Start/finish: Car park overlooking Coumeenoole Bay along the R559 at **V 317**80 **974**50.

Distance: 14.5km/9 miles **Total Ascent:** 600m/1,969ft
Walking Time: 5 to 6 hours
Maps: OSi Sheet 70 **Walk Grade:** 3

Rising on eagle's wings

The car park offers splendid views out to sea and towards Dunmore Head and the cliffs at Carrignaparka. Facing inland, turn right and head south along the R559 toward Slea Head. After 65m or so, there is a grassy ramp leading uphill beyond a metal gate and stile by a Yellow Man signpost. Leave the R559 here and follow the waymarked path, which is part of the Dingle Way, steeply uphill.

After about 600m along the path, the ground starts to level and reaches a cairn sitting atop a boulder. Cross the stile by a stone wall and fence at **V 318**96 **970**72, then turn left immediately to head uphill. Keep the stone wall and fence to your left. The slope is moderately steep and mainly on short grass with the occasional clump of heather and bracken. After a rocky section, the path passes under electric lines and then becomes grassy again.

Pass three stone enclosures after a gap in the wall. Continue to follow the wall upslope, which is interspersed with another stone enclosure, until it ends. A firm path then leads uphill through an area of scattered rocks and heather. The slope relents when reaching a

Mount Eagle

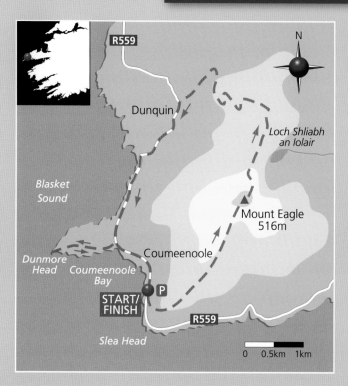

Dunmore Head, Blasket Sound and Great Blasket Island as seen from the western slopes of Mount Eagle.

cairn at Binn an Choma (point 424m) with a stone circle beneath at **V 327**76 **979**88. Continue uphill beyond the cairn where the stone wall reappears.

Fabulous views towards the sea open up during the ascent. To the west, a collection of islands adorns the blue waters beyond the broad pointed finger of Dunmore Head. The largest of these is Great Blasket Island, with a scattered group of smaller islands, including Beginish, to its north. Further away still from the Great Blasket are the islands of Inishtooskert, Tearaght, Inishnabro and Inishvickillane. Millennia ago, the high points of the islands of Great Blasket, Inishnabro and Inishvickillane once belonged to the same mountain range, instead of being the separate land masses that they are today.

The slope eases and becomes increasingly peaty, with a covering of moor grass and sphagnum moss. Veer northeast to reach the summit trig point of Mount Eagle at **V 334**67 **989**47 where sweeping panoramas of land and sea unfold.

The city of Fahan and Hollywood films

Further down the southeast slopes of Mount Eagle lies the townland of Fahan. The hillside here is decorated with clochans – drystone huts in the shape of beehives and thick walls – dating to the early Middle Ages. The ruins of hundreds of these huts prompted one nineteenth-century antiquarian to call the area the 'city of Fahan'.

Leave the summit and descend northeast to the edge of the plateau at **V 335**96 **990**91 for views of the corrie lake, Eagle Lough. Follow the spur downhill in a northerly direction until reaching a track about 200m away. Continue to descend along the track for just under 1.5km until it bends at **Q 338**75 **004**26. Veer left along the bend as it zigzags down the mountainside to eventually reach a tarmac road. *Cruach Mhárthain* (403m/1,322ft), rising like a brown pap, dominates the view northwards during the descent. The now-demolished village of Kirarry that featured in the film *Ryan's Daughter* was built on its slopes. Further west from *Cruach Mhárthain*, at Clogher Head, director Ron Howard built his set for *Far and Away* in 1991.

Dunmore Head and the Spanish Armada

Turn left and walk down the tarmac to reach a T-junction. Turn left here and continue along the R559, passing the townlands of Glebe and Ballyickeen. The sea is to your immediate right until reaching the land mass of Dunmore Head. At this point, continue along the R559 for around 500m until reaching a narrow tarmac lane to the right at its southern end.

Turn right and walk along this lane for around 250m. Shortly after a car park, leave the tarmac and hop carefully across a fence on the right into a field. Head uphill on the grassy slope using an informal path until reaching a flat grassy area. Pass a ruined building and head westwards down the slope for around 200m until the ground starts to fall away steeply into Blasket Sound. There is an Ogham Stone – an upright stone bearing inscriptions of primitive Irish writing – in the vicinity. The stack of Liúir and some rock slabs can also be seen out to sea. Veer right to descend a steeper slope and continue to its tip at **V 301**50 **980**50 to reach the most westernmost point of the Dingle Peninsula and mainland Ireland.

There are fine views of the whaleback hump of Great Blasket Island separated by Blasket Sound. Stop here to reflect on the events that transpired centuries ago on a stormy day in September 1588, when ships of the Spanish Armada were steered through Blasket Sound. Two of the ships managed to get to safety. However, one, the *Santa Maria de la Rosa*, charged out of control through the Sound and collided with other ships. The ship foundered in the Sound and hundreds of Spaniards drowned, including a prince, whose body was eventually laid to rest in an old burial ground in Dunquin.

From here, retrace steps back to the R559 and continue for just over a 1km to reach the car park at Coumeenoole at the start.

The intricate Dingle coastline as seen from high on the western slopes of Mount Eagle.

WALK 2: THE MODEST GEM OF DINGLE

The glorious panorama of Mount Eagle, Cruach Mhárthain *and Smerwick Harbour, looking west from Reenconnell's broad summit ridge.*

The hill of Reenconnell (274m/899ft) rises above the townland of Kilmalkedar in the western end of the Dingle Peninsula, east of Murreagh. For its modest height, its grassy summit ridge gives wonderful views of the entire Brandon range to the east and a panorama of rolling hills and the sea to the west. This is the easiest walk of the entire Dingle Peninsula in this guidebook. It is suitable as a simple hike for beginners or a family with children, or as a short romantic stroll to admire the sunrise or sunset.

Start/finish: Along a laneway by Kilmalkedar church and graveyard at **Q 402**03 **061**90.

Distance: 3.5km/2.2 miles **Total Ascent:** 205m/673ft
Walking Time: 1 to 1½ hours
Maps: OSi Sheet 70 **Walk Grade:** 1

Kilmalkedar church and the Saints' Road

Kilmalkedar is an ancient church site on the Dingle Peninsula that was probably founded by St Maolcethair in the seventh century. The present church, however, was built in the mid-twelfth century and displays an architecture essentially Irish Romanesque in style, with its

Reenconnell Hill

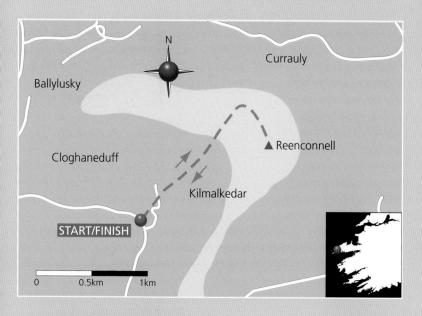

Ballylusky

Currauly

Cloghaneduff

▲ Reenconnell

Kilmalkedar

START/FINISH

0   0.5km   1km

Kilmalkedar church and graveyard.

chevrons and diamond shapes. There is a sixth-century standing stone inside the church carved with the Latin alphabet, a small cross and the letters 'DNI'. Outside the church is a graveyard; its front section has an early sundial, a large stone cross and an ogham stone (a standing stone with a series of slashes carved across its edge. The slashes relate to a primitive alphabet system dating back to the fourth century. Ogham is named after Ogma, the Celtic god of eloquence).

From the start point near the church, walk northeast along the lane with the graveyard on the right, then follow a Yellow 'Saint' signpost up a stony track that eventually bends left at a metal gate. Shortly after, there is a sliding metal gate on the right. Go through this gate, continue to follow the signposts and enter a green field at **Q 403**27 **063**07, which is normally full of sheep. This route is part of the *Cosán na Naomh*, or 'the road of the Saints', a 18km/11 mile pilgrim route that links the ancient Christian sites on the Dingle Peninsula. At the far end of the field is a ladder stile at **Q 404**78 **064**44 that leads to another field with drystone walls on either side. Climb over this stile and then immediately veer left to surmount yet another ladder stile that provides access to the next field.

A panorama of panoramas

Once in this field, continue on uphill, keeping the wall and fence on the right, to eventually reach a ladder stile and a metal gate. The ascent is a gradual one beyond this on a grassy path flanked by clumps of compact rush, patches of gorse and by a wall on its far right. Walk uphill for about a distance of 400m and come to another ladder stile and a metal gate at **Q 407**18 **066**85. The wall on the right is now heavily covered in heather and gorse. Keep following the yellow-marked signposts to the col where there is a step stile at **Q 411**46 **071**25.

Bear right here, with a drystone wall also on the right, in a general southeast direction. After about 300m, the wall intersects a fence corner at **Q 413**05 **069**09. Get over it carefully without damaging the wall, using wooden posts to maintain balance. If unable to, then go no further, as the view from here is no different than that from the summit. However, if you can, then walk a short distance away beyond the wall to the highest point of Reenconnell at **Q 413**26 **068**00.

The view from the col and all along the grassy ridge towards the summit of Reenconnell is all-encompassing – a priceless gem. I fondly recall how much it took me by surprise and being impressed by it during my first wander to these heights some years back. The entire

The southern end of Smerwick Harbour and the brown pap of Cruach Mhárthain rising beyond dominate the view west from the col near Reenconnell.

Brandon range, from Masatiompan (763m/2,503ft) to Ballysitteragh (623m/2,044ft), sweeps the view to the east. To the west, gentle hills – Mount Eagle (516m/1,693ft) to the far left and the pointed *Cruach Mhárthain* (403m/1,322ft) to its right – rise beyond the broad arm of Smerwick Harbour and the rolling landscape of the peninsula. On the western end of Smerwick Harbour sits *Dún an Óir*, the 'fort of gold'. It was here in 1580 that 600 Irish and Spanish who gave themselves up to Elizabeth I's forces were brutally massacred.

After enjoying the views and perhaps also a picnic, retrace steps back to Kilmalkedar and the start point of the walk.

The gentle western slopes of the Brandon range seen from the summit of Reenconnell.

WALK 3: SENTINEL BY THE SEA

At the edge of the Atlantic on the Dingle Peninsula is a mountain that rises like a sentinel above the sea. This peak, Masatiompan (763m/2,503ft), marks the start of the ridge that extends southwards, over *Piaras Mór* (748m/2,454ft), and then towards a mountain named after St Brendan, a fifth- to sixth-century monastic saint. This walk is a fine mix of mountains and sea, and serves as the perfect introduction to the Brandon group of hills.

Start/finish: Large car park at a cul-de-sac at **Q 433**68 **124**68.

Distance: 10km/6.2 miles ***Total Ascent:*** 800m/2,625ft
Walking Time: 3³⁄₄ to 4³⁄₄ hours
Maps: OSi Sheet 70 ***Walk Grade:*** 3

Of monks and voyages

The car park at the start of the walk overlooks Brandon Creek where St Brendan set sail in a small leather curragh with a band of pilgrims to seek out the Promised Land fifteen centuries ago. From the car park, head northeast, going through a metal gate. Walk along a stony track, following Yellow Man signposts and pass a further two metal gates. After the second metal gate at **Q 444**65 **135**79, bear left, to eventually pass an area of turf-cutting. Now ascend the slopes northwards to a peaty col where a plunging view of the sea and cliffs is suddenly revealed, overlooking a line of fence. The spur leading to *Cnoc na mBristí* lies ahead, and beyond that is the steep mountainside that rises from the sea at Brandon Head to the summit of Masatiompan.

While ascending the moderate grassy slopes up the spur, gaze towards the brownish-green landscape due south. It is said that once a community of monks lived and farmed in fields around here, so much so that the area is locally known as *Fothar na Manach* or 'field of the monks'. Continue along until nearing the top of the spur below some rocky outcrops. Cross a fence at its corner (**Q 449**44 **138**22) beside a small 'fang' of rock in order to arrive at the top of the spur,

Masatiompan

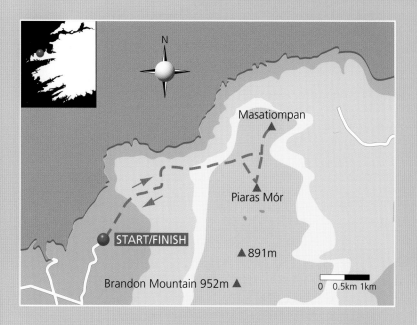

Masatiompan

Piaras Mór

START/FINISH

▲ 891m

Brandon Mountain 952m ▲

0   0.5km 1km

Looking eastwards along the spur leading to Cnoc na mBristí, *and the steep mountainside that soars from the sea to the summit of Masatiompan above.*

Looking down onto Beennaman, Brandon Creek and Beenmore from Cnoc na mBristí.

where there are fine views back down to Beennaman (378m/1,240ft), Brandon Creek and Smerwick Harbour. Beyond this, the slope relents and eventually reaches a metal gate and the Yellow Man sign at **Q 453**62 **138**44.

Ogham stone, ring fort and summits above the sea

Go through the gate and keep following the track, part of the Dingle Way, that rises gradually to the col at **Q 464**90 **141**20. A band of dark-grey rock guards Masatiompan's southwest slopes above on the left as you near the col. On reaching the col, you may want to investigate the opposite side of fence where there is an ogham stone bearing an inscription. Returning to the col, keep the fence on the right and ascend a rocky and mossy slope following the fence until reaching a small pile of rocks with a standing stone on the summit of Masatiompan at **Q 465**36 **145**48.

Take a short detour and descend northeast, beyond a step stile to reach a Red Man marker at the edge of a slope at **Q 465**88 **145**98 before it starts to fall steeply down the mountainside. You are now standing on slopes high above Brandon Head, and the view eastwards is breathtaking. The arc of Sauce Creek, a deep, sheltered cove, can be seen poking inland just beyond it. Steep mountainside rises above Sauce Creek and its brownish upper slopes extend eastwards to Brandon Point. The curved arm of Brandon Bay lies further still with the mountains of the eastern end of the Dingle Peninsula inland.

Retrace steps back to the summit of Masatiompan, and then descend back down to the col. From the col, ascend in a general southerly direction to pass a ring fort, and later gain the summit of *Piaras Mór* at **Q 463**81 **136**52, which is marked by a small cairn on a jumble of rocky outcrops. There are excellent views of Brandon Mountain and the Faha ridge to the south, and back towards Masatiompan.

Leave the summit of *Piaras Mór* and walk down grassy slopes to re-emerge on the track at **Q 460**33 **140**57, following Yellow Man signs back to the start point and passing six metal gates along the way.

The rump of Masatiompan as seen from Piaras Mór.

WALK 4: BRANDON MOUNTAIN

Brandon Mountain (952m/3,123ft) or *Cnoc Bréanainn* is one of my favourite Irish summits. It is the highest point in Ireland outside the chain of peaks that dominate the MacGillycuddy's Reeks. There is an other-worldly quality on its lofty heights, and in particular along its ridge that takes in two other summits: Brandon Peak (840m/2,756ft) and Gearhane (803m/2,634ft). It is common for this mountain range to 'wear its cap' on cloudy days, but on a clear day, views of mountain, lake, land and sea from its summit ridge are unparalleled. Here are two options to explore these heights: one from its more interesting eastern side from Faha and another via an easier route up its western flanks.

Option A – The eastern approach

Start: The car park at a cul-de-sac (**Q 493**82 **119**62) at Faha, a townland on slopes above the village of Cloghane. **Finish:** Leave a second car at around **Q 470**50 **069**00 or parked somewhere along the road marked as 'The Pilgrims' Route' on the OSi map. Otherwise, it is a long walk on tarmac (about 8km/5 miles) back to the car park at Faha.

Distance: 10km/6.2 miles, based on the two grid locations given above.
Total Ascent: 980m/3,215ft **Walking Time:** 4 to 5 hrs
Maps: OSi Sheet 70 **Walk Grade:** 4

Crashes, explosions and trapped lakes

A 'Going Climbing?' and 'The Country Code' signboard catches the eye at the car park. Walk to a metal gate, passing the signs for 'Mt Brandon' and the Yellow Man, go through a wooden gate and up a grassy ramp towards the Grotto, crossing a metal ladder stile and a small metal gate on the way. Walk along a stony path with patches of gorse, passing just under the Grotto. Cross some wooden step stiles, following white metal posts, then walk through a gap in the fence. Continue this uphill progress on the path until just below the Faha ridge at **Q 481**74 **120**36. The Faha ridge and Brandon Mountain are the site of several aircraft crashes in the 1940s. One aircraft, the *Condor*, belly-

Brandon Mountain

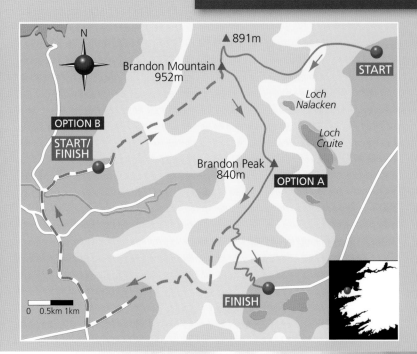

- ▲891m
- Brandon Mountain 952m
- START
- Loch Nalacken
- Loch Cruite
- OPTION B
- START/FINISH
- OPTION A
- Brandon Peak 840m
- FINISH
- 0   0.5km 1km

The view northwards back to Brandon Mountain from its summit ridge.
The Faha ridge extends to the right in the distance.

landed on top of the Faha ridge in 1940: four crew members suffered broken limbs while two emerged unscathed. Another aircraft, carrying six Polish squadron members involved in hunting U-boats, crashed and exploded on the slopes of Brandon Mountain in 1943.

Contour along under the slopes of Faha, following the path until the white posts end around **Q 476**12 **114**85. At this point, note that the coniferous plantation as indicated on the OSi map no longer exists. There are splashes of yellow paint daubed on rock, marking the path ahead, and it becomes littered with boulders.

The path becomes firmer underfoot as it bends inwards around **Q 470**70 **115**52, winding its way under the rocky sandstone crags of the mighty Faha ridge towering above. In the valley below on the left, the Paternoster Lakes come into sight. This is a series of lakes under the steep eastern side of the Brandon range strung together like rosary beads: the largest is *Loch Cruite* ('harp lake'), followed by *Loch Nalacken* ('duck lake'), and then a group of smaller lakes nestled in rocky shelves leading up the valley. It is a lovely setting.

Between sea and sky

In the mist, the following grid locations will be helpful as you enter the boulder-filled amphitheatre of a bare rocky glen of sheer walls and scree slopes carved during the Ice Age: **Q 465**04 **118**52 (there is a yellow arrow on rock) and **Q 463**45 **118**14 (there is yellow paint on rock). From here, walk south of a small tarn to the bottom of a cliff at **Q 461**65 **118**32. The path swings right here up a very steep (the use of hands may be required) but straightforward gully leading to a col at the top of the ridge (**Q 460**58 **120**45).

Once you reach the top, a striking vision of mountain and sea greets you. Continue left (southwards) up a moderate slope leading to the summit of Brandon Mountain at **Q 460**46 **116**05 with its cairn, trig point, fence posts and a cross on a pile of rock. The remains of St Brendan's Oratory and a holy well are also said to mark the summit. In pre-Christian times, the summit was a site of Celtic harvest celebrations.

The view from Brandon Mountain is a dreamland of mountain panoramas: the imposing Faha ridge close at hand; the majestic line of mountain running north to south; the intricate coastline westwards with views of Smerwick Harbour, The Three Sisters, Great Blasket Island and a scattering of other islands; the curved arc of Brandon Bay to the east and the mountains of the rest of the peninsula; and lovely valleys and moorland to the west.

Looking southeast from the slopes of Brandon Mountain to its magnificent fang-like ridge that extends to Brandon Peak.

The Paternoster Lakes, the eastern end of the Faha ridge, Brandon Bay and the eastern hills of the Dingle Peninsula as seen from Brandon Mountain.

A ridge walk to remember

The next 3km or so are an exhilarating ridge walk. The ridge can be seen snaking southeast like a prehistoric reptile with sharp, angular fins; with its eastern side plunging down into the depths of the Paternoster chain like a yawning abyss. Staying a safe distance away from this steep side, descend in a southeasterly direction to meet a wall, fence post and a path at **Q 463**03 **113**82, which later crosses the wall at **Q 463**67 **113**14. Continue on the ridge southeast, and then south, leaving it only at around **Q 470**00 **096**00 for a stiff pull up to the summit of Brandon Peak: on its top look back along the ridge you traversed. After savouring this and other views from the fang-shaped summit, which are just as good as from Brandon Mountain, descend southwestwards, with the grassy ridge narrowing just before the top of Gearhane. Continue on: there is a Green Man sign at **Q 468**24 **087**73 on southern slopes below Gearhane marking St Brendan's way, along with a gate and a fence.

Descend downhill on moorland to meet a track at **Q 463**54 **081**20. Turn left once on the track, following a series of zigzags down into the valley of Mullaghveal, with the small lake of *Loch na mBan* visible in the distance on the right during the descent. A green road is reached and this eventually passes a ruined stone-walled dwelling on the right. The track meanders to near a stream to the left, and zigzags down to meet a metal gate at **Q 467**83 **069**16. Here, turn left onto a main track that leads to the finish at **Q 470**50 **069**00.

Option B – The western approach

Start/finish: A large car park at **Q 433**90 **094**33 at the end of a cul-de-sac signposted 'Mt Brandon' on the western side of the mountain.

Distance: 7km/4.3 miles ***Total Ascent:*** 780m/2,559ft
Walking Time: 3 to 3¾ hours ***Maps:*** OSi Sheet 70
Walk Grade: 2 to 3

In the footsteps of Saints

A board at the car park describes the *Cosán na Naomh* ('Path of the Saints'), an old pilgrimage road linked with St Brendan. There is also a new stone memorial dedicated to 'people who followed in the path of St Brendan for the cure of cancer' at the car park. At the end of the car park, cross the bridge over the stream and follow the track uphill with the river now on the left until reaching a metal gate with a swinging metal gate on its right. Go through this and continue on for a distance of 100m or so until **Q 437**20 **096**47. At this point, veer left, away from the green track and follow wooden (white) posts, crossing a stream to a pile of rocks with a wooden cross in the centre at **Q 438**97 **098**64.

With the stream now on the right, continue to follow the white posts uphill on a grassy path to another pile of rocks marked by a cross: this is the First Station on the *Cosán na Naomh*. The track passes two other Stations, becomes peaty and stony until reaching a standing stone with a small pile of rocks beside a white post near the Fourth Station. The track becomes even stonier after this and the slope steepens and becomes rockier until reaching the next Station. The slope flattens somewhat after this, reaching a standing stone on a rocky mound before reaching the Sixth Station. The route progresses uphill from here, charting its way along a further eight Stations. It passes an area of rocky outcrops splattered on the grassy slope, winds along the side of a spur, and then meets a wall before the final pull up to the summit of Brandon Mountain.

Once at the summit, retrace steps back to the car park at the start.

Longer Variation: It is possible to continue from Brandon Mountain along the ridge, taking in Brandon Peak and Gearhane along the way, and reaching the Green Man sign at **Q 468**24 **087**73 as in Option A. From here descend southwestwards, then swing south along a boggy plateau to arrive at a track at **Q 457**50 **067**50 just before the col. Follow the track, marked on the OSi map as 'The Pilgrims' Route', as it meanders down the western flanks on the mountain above Glin North until eventually reaching a lane. Continue southwest down this lane until reaching a junction. Turn right at the junction and walk along the minor road, taking a right at the fork at **Q 421**00 **083**50 and then a right again at the signpost for Mt Brandon back to the start point at the cul-de-sac (**Q 433**90 **094**33). For this variation, add a further 12km/7.5 miles to the distance and 3 to 4 hours to the approximate walking time.

WALK 5: UNDER THE SHADOW OF BRANDON

This is a short, straightforward route of stunning contrasts. The route goes from the top of the Conor Pass down into a wide, lonely valley with ancient field systems, ruined stone dwellings and mysterious lakes. As you walk along blanket bog, russet heather-clad slopes and the soft summits of Ballysitteragh (623m/2,044ft), Beennabrack (600m/1,968ft) and *An Bhinn Dubh* (478m/1,568ft) you are always under the shadow of mighty Brandon.

Start/finish: The highest point on the Conor Pass Road at **Q 490**41 **055**83, where there are spaces for many cars.

Distance: 11km/6.8 miles **Total Ascent:** 610m/2,001ft
Walking Time: 3¾ to 4¾ hours **Maps:** OSi Sheet 70
Walk Grade: 3

Walk down the road as it winds its way along a narrow section under the Maughanablagher Cliffs. About 1km down the road, notice a metal gate on the left at **Q 498**22 **059**94. This gate leads to a grassy, stony track that zigzags down the hillside into the Cloghane Valley where several lakes sit. After an area littered with small boulders, you will soon arrive at some ruined stone dwellings, surrounded by drystone-walled fields at **Q 490**70 **064**10.

This is an area where sheep roam and ravens soar in the sky. The boulder-strewn slopes are decorated with bracken, sphagnum moss, star moss and compact rush near the waters edge of Clogharee Lough.

Walk to the northeastern end of the lake where there is a fence at **Q 490**29 **066**11. Here, stag horn lichen grows amongst the moor grass and clumps of ling heather. Follow the water's edge. About 150m away you will reach another fence: cross it at a low gap at **Q 488**93 **067**43. Later cross a stream to a field lined with moor grass, ling heather and gorse. Continue walking northwestwards to reach a bend at another stream. Cross this, and you will arrive at a green track at **Q 485**94 **070**11.

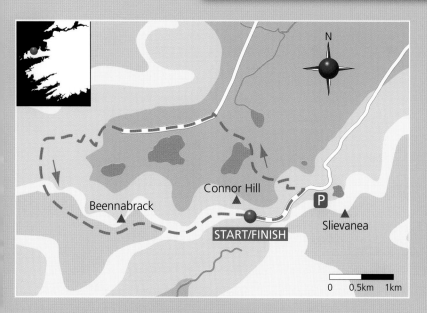

Ballysitteragh, Beennabrack and *An Bhinn Dubh*

N

Beennabrack ▲

Connor Hill ▲

START/FINISH ●

P

Slievanea ▲

0   0.5km   1km

Ruined stone dwellings near Clogharee Lough, with the Brandon range beyond.

The striated eastern cliffs of Ballysitteragh.

There is a metal gate at the end of the track. On the right of the gate, by a section of drystone wall, there is a portion of fence with a wooden stile of sorts. You are now on the section of road known as The Pilgrims' Route. Follow the road westwards towards Mullaghveal. The tarmac ends after about 1.5km of road, near the farmhouse on the left.

The Pilgrims' Route now becomes a track that leads westwards to the obvious col above. Go through six gates, some accompanied by stiles, along the track as it zigzags up the slope. The predominantly grassy track becomes increasingly stony, as you walk under some electricity poles just before the col.

Next, walk to the corner of some fences at **Q 457**91 **067**25. Cross the fence there and ascend southwards on the grassy and mossy slope, keeping the line of fences to your left. Midway up, the spur veers southeastwards. Continue following the fence line to the grassy plateau adorned with wood-rush and stag horn lichen.

As you approach the summit of Ballysitteragh, veer away from the fence to reach a pile of rocks at **Q 460**55 **057**16. For a flat summit, Ballysitteragh offers amazing 360° views of the Dingle Peninsula, and especially that of Dingle town, harbour and bay to the south.

From Ballysitteragh, walk southeastwards towards a broad col. There is a fence corner at **Q 463**71 **055**55. Continue following the fence to the summit of Beennabrack, and then eastwards down a col, followed by a slight rise to *An Bhinn Dubh* ('the Black Peak') before descending to meet the Conor Pass Road again.

In the 1950s, a child's body was found in the peat, completely preserved. She is believed to be from the seventh or eighth century. She had red hair, wore a dress and held a purse in her hand.

Looking across the Mullaghveal Valley to Brandon Peak from the slopes of Ballysitteragh.

WALK 6: DINGLE'S BEST-KEPT SECRET

The next three walks explore the hills of central Dingle. We start off with a fine circuit of rich variety above and beyond the Glennahoo Valley, initially over a group of hills over 400m: Beenbo (474m/1,555ft), Slievenagower (484m/1,588ft) and Slievenalecka (456m/1,496ft). These modest, unfrequented summits provide fascinating views of hidden north-facing coums. The route then explores some remote lakes surrounded by cliffs deep in the heart of the mountains. The summit of *An Cnapán Mór* (649m/2,129ft) is visited before a long hike across featureless terrain towards the secluded corner of Maghanaboe.

Start/finish: Parking spaces at Ballyduff or *An Baile Dubh* graveyard at **Q 540**70 **101**00, due east of the village of Cloghane.

Distance: 17km/10.6 miles **Total Ascent:** 900m/2,953ft
Walking Time: 5¾ to 7 hours **Maps:** OSi Sheet 70
Walk Grade: 4

The Beenbo ridge

The townland of *An Baile Dubh* is associated with the Celtic deity Crom Dubh, a god of fertility and harvest. During the Iron Age, the ancient Celts would celebrate a harvest ritual known as *Domhnach Crom Dubh*, in honour of Crom Dubh.

From the graveyard, walk southeastwards along the minor road for about 100m until it forks. Take the right fork and walk up the lane, which is flanked by gorse bushes on both sides, until it takes a right bend. There is a small rusted metal gate about 100m away at **Q 540**47 **095**04 leading into a field. Turn left and go through this gate, followed by another shortly after, keeping a line of fences to your right.

Continue up the grassy slope, crossing two fences with care, to arrive at point 298m on top of the spur. There is a track on the other side of the fence below the grassy crest on its western end. However, it is more rewarding to keep to the left of fence and traverse the ridge leading southwards to Beenbo.

Beenbo, Slievenagower and Slievenalecka

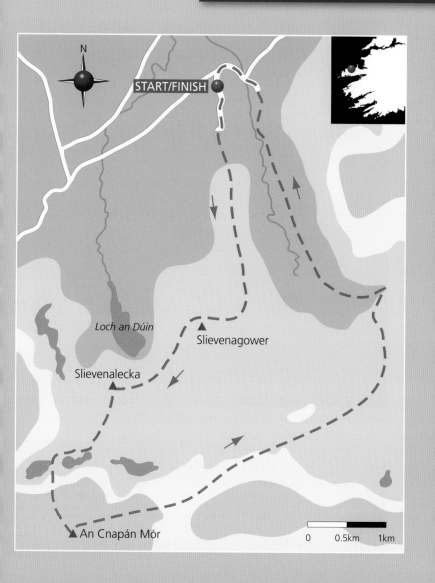

N

START/FINISH

Loch an Dúin

▲ Slievenagower

Slievenalecka

▲ An Cnapán Mór

0   0.5km   1km

Looking down the grassy ridge of Ballyduff, with Brandon Bay beyond.

The ridge, also marked as Ballyduff or *An Baile Dubh* on the OSi map, is mainly grassy with some rock outcrops. It is narrow in places, but always manageable. As you ascend, the northern end of a beak-shaped range of hills opens up on your right. The Glennahoo River can also be seen twisting and turning for miles in the deep-cut valley below on your left. As you near the top of the ridge, look back at the way you came for fine views down its crest and also of Brandon Bay behind.

The grassy and mossy summit of Beenbo at **Q 545**39 **074**59 is unmarked. Interestingly, its Irish equivalent on the OSi map is *Gob an Iolair*, or 'eagle's beak' – a translation that does not match up with its anglicised version. Beenbo sounds more like *Binn Bó* or 'peak of the cattle', which seems to relate to the other place names of the area: for instance, Maghanaboe or *Macha na Bó* in the valley below meaning 'plain of the cattle'. However, when viewed from the sky, Beenbo does resemble an eagle's beak, so I'll give the OSi the benefit of the doubt!

Dingle's finest view

Descend southwestwards from Beenbo and cross a fence at the col to rise again to the summit of Slievenagower, the 'mountain of the goat', akin to Ben Gower in the Twelve Bens of Connemara. There is no cairn at its highest point at **Q 539**60 **072**26.

Carry on westwards from the summit for some 250m to the edge of a steep heather-clad slope at **Q 536**71 **071**40 to be greeted by one of the finest views on the entire Dingle Peninsula. The blue lake of *Loch an Dúin* stretches out for nearly 1km below you, with a green island just off its centre. Slievenalecka and Slievanea's Northeast Top project sharply skywards beyond the lake, and the entire Brandon ridge sweeps the skyline in the distance.

Next, descend southwestwards down rugged slopes, aiming for a col. There is a stone shelter near the col, and a waterfall plunging down

The view from Slievenagower across Loch an Dúin *to Slievenalecka and Slievanea Northeast Top.*

the valley below also comes into view. Cross a stream at the rugged gap at **Q 534**11 **065**32 and ascend the slopes ahead, keeping a line of fences to your right, to the summit of Slievenalecka (*An Starraicín*, 'the steeple') at **Q 527**77 **064**11.

Hidden lakes

Descend southwestwards from Slievenalecka on rough moorland and an area of peat hags for a distance of about 800m to *Loch Meáin*, one of the Coumanare lakes. Walk along the rocky northern end of *Loch Meáin* to a waterway that connects it to *Loch Iarthair*. A good spot to stop for lunch is at **Q 520**17 **055**38 on a rocky and grassy patch just above the waters of *Loch Iarthair*. This is an area of silence and solitude. The lakes sit in a remote hollow flanked by fearsome cliffs to the south and steep slopes to the west.

Our objective is a prominent spur between the two lakes, due south. Cross the waterway and ascend the rocky spur, weaving around rock slabs and along grassy ledges. Throngs of fir club moss grace the slopes. The wild, lake-strewn landscape below is impressive.

Ascend the steep, grassy slope until its gradient eases near the top of the plateau. Aim for the obvious highest point ahead, due southeast. It gets stony near the summit of the big lump of *An Cnapán Mór*, where a trig point and a cairn on a pile of rocks greet you at **Q 522**26 **045**90. Views to the south of Dingle Bay across to the Iveragh Peninsula are good.

Descent to the 'plain of the cattle'

From the summit, descend eastwards on moderate, stony slopes that later become grassy. Meet a stony track about 1.5km away at **Q 536**96 **050**13, just north of the col at Windy Gap. Follow this track for another 1.3km until it peters out around a broad gap at **Q 548**93 **057**10.

Here, keep the high ground to your left and contour under it, aiming for the lower ground southwest of summit 383m just over 1km away. There are traces of a faint path at times, but it is mainly trackless, grassy and stony terrain. The rough ground drops steadily around **Q 556**78 **058**78, and here aim northeastwards for a distance of 500m to reach a flat grassy area.

At **Q 560**17 **062**43, it starts to rise again. There is a group of rocks scattered amongst an area of tussocks, compact rush and heather. Keep higher ground to your right and contour underneath. When you are just under summit 383m, veer northwards to meet some black posts at **Q 561**77 **069**67.

Follow the path to a Red Man signpost at **Q 560**45 **072**07 overlooking the top of the Maghanaboe Valley. A delightful track cuts diagonally across its yellow-brown slopes, above a ravine below and leading towards a notch in its northeastern corner at **Q 562**50 **076**41. Here, several streams cut deeply into a rock fault tumble down the slopes. This is a fabulous spot: the comforting melody of cascades, the gentle hum of the cool breeze and the almost artistically shaped rock shelves.

The track now leads westwards down into the Maghanaboe Valley, where cattle once grazed. You now walk down the northern end of the ravine, as the stream cuts its way sharply down the pear-yellow hillside. Holly trees adorn its sides, along with strings of fraughan and clumps of St Patrick's cabbage. Common violets, yellow tormentils and pale yellow primroses also bloom here in spring.

As the track veers right, leading northwestwards out of the valley, you will arrive above some ruined stone cottages surrounded by stone walls at **Q 556**34 **075**30. According to tradition, the Dineens and the O'Donnells eked out a living here in the nineteenth century. It is also believed that its last occupant was Mary 'Macha na Bó' – an old lady with long flowing white hair who yelled at hikers, but on some occasions took them in for a cup of tea.

From here, it is a simple walk along the track on the valley floor beside the twisting Glennahoo River and under mountainous slopes clothed in great sweeps of scree for some 2.5km to reach a junction at **Q 546**11 **100**84. At the junction turn left, and then left again on the main road, before finally turning left once more into *An Baile Dubh* back to the start point.

Descending into the Maghanaboe Valley.

33

WALK 7: IN THE FOOTSTEPS OF LEGENDS

The village of Anascaul has a pub called the South Pole Inn, aptly named in connection with Tom Crean, a local man. Crean, who coincidentally shares his birthday with Sir Edmund Hillary, was enlisted with the Royal Navy just before his 16th birthday and played a heroic role in the ill-fated 1911–13 Scott expedition to the South Pole. He also participated in the 1914–16 *Endurance* expedition to the Antarctic with Shackleton, which included an epic five-month journey over ice, ocean and land after their ship was trapped in pack ice and sank. Upon retiring in 1920, Crean returned to his local village, married and ran the South Pole Inn. This walk explores the hills of Crean's backyard, in a picturesque valley flanked by steep cliffs at Lough Anscaul. It is one of my favourite areas in the Dingle Peninsula, with the valley and mountains steeped in legends. Two summits are visited in this lovely walk: *Cnoc Mhaoilionáin* (593m/1,946ft) and *An Bhánóg Thuaidh* (641m/2,103ft).

Start/finish: Just west of the South Pole Inn at Anascaul village, turn right after a bridge onto a minor road signposted 'Anascaul Lake'. Follow this and take a right upon reaching a crossroad. Drive to its end, pass through gates and park at spaces near Lough Anscaul at **Q 582**48 **051**09, just below the rock-strewn slopes, precipitous cliffs and gullies of Carrigblagher.

Distance: 10km/6.2 miles ***Total Ascent:*** 650m/2,133ft
Walking Time: 3½ to 4½ hours *Maps:* OSi Sheet 70
Walk Grade: 4

Cúchulainn and the giant

Walk back a distance of just over 400m southwards along the road to **Q 582**98 **047**17. At present, there is a fence that zigzags up the green slopes on your right. A stream flows down beside it. Keep the fence and stream to your left and ascend southwestwards up the gradual, grassy slope. There are traces of a faint path leading to a clump of gorse about a distance of 150m up the hill at **Q 581**76 **046**93.

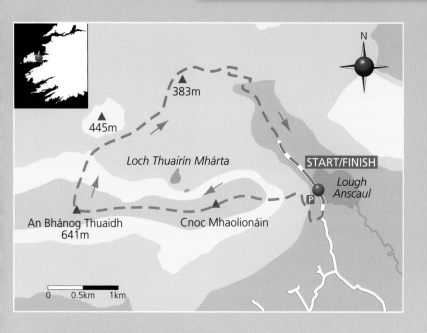

Lough Anscaul and
Cnoc Mhaoilionáin

383m

445m

Loch Thuairín Mhárta

START/FINISH

Lough Anscaul

An Bhánog Thuaidh
641m

Cnoc Mhaolionáin

0   0.5km   1km

N

*Looking northeastwards from near the top of the Carrigblagher Cliffs towards
the back of the Anascaul Valley, with Beenoskee towering behind.*

Lough Anscaul, Reamore and Dromavally as seen from the Cnoc Mhaoilionáin *spur.*

Here veer northwestwards, zigzagging up the moderately steep slopes and follow the line of the Carrigblagher Cliffs (while keeping a safe distance from the edge). The grassy and rocky slope, although sustained, is always manageable, and at times there is evidence of a trodden path. The valley below starts to open up as you ascend higher, but the best view overall is at the eastern end of the spur at **Q 579**48 **050**72.

The entire valley at the back of Lough Anscaul, with the Garrivagh River twisting and turning, can be appreciated. Beenoskee (826m/2,710ft) towers above the sharp cliffs of Reamore to the north. Lough Anscaul itself appears like a giant dark-blue carpet far down below, resting by the fertile slopes of Dromavally.

The panoramic view from Cnoc Mhaoilionáin's slopes includes all the hills of central Dingle and the Brandon range to the northwest.

Lough Anscaul is named after Scál Ní Mhurnáin, one of Cúchulainn's many women. Scál was taken captive by a giant and held at the lake. Cúchulainn charged up the high ground of Reamore and hurled fiery boulders at the giant, who stood where you stand now. The flurry of boulders progressed until Cúchulainn suddenly gave a loud groan. Scál presumed her lover was killed, and in sorrow she drowned herself in the lake.

A large pile of standing stones with a collapsed inner chamber graces the flat high ground northeast of Reamore, probably a Bronze Age burial mound for noble tribesmen.

'Oh there are mountains, there are mountains everywhere'

Next, ascend the straightforward spur leading westwards towards *Cnoc Mhaoilionáin*, and perhaps steal a look behind to catch a glimpse of the fine view down the slopes. There is a cairn at the top of the spur at **Q 572**69 **050**47, and from here undulating terrain leads you to the twin cairns on the summit of *Cnoc Mhaoilionáin* at **Q 568**15 **048**84. The mountains of the Dingle Peninsula will fill your scope of vision to the west, north and east on the summit. Dingle Bay will also hold you in its spell and across its waters the peaks of the MacGillycuddy's Reeks can be made out on a clear day.

From here, simply follow the broad ridge westwards. The terrain is of mixed grass and peat and there is a good trodden path. It is a pleasant stroll on the undulating ridge with wonderful all-round views. A line of posts follows the ridge line, and later you will cross some fences to arrive at a peaty area above two lakes, with the range of hills from Glennahoo to Stradbally Mountain figuring prominently

in the background. A broad col then leads to slopes that rise to a mossy and stony summit area, culminating with a small pile of rocks at **Q 548**30 **048**27 marking the top of *An Bhánóg Thuaidh*.

The view from this summit is similar to the previous one. However, particularly impressive is the vista across the Owenmore Valley towards the sharp eastern side of Brandon, with *Loch Cruite* and the Paternoster route in full sight.

From the summit of *An Bhánóg Thuaidh* set a course northwards, then veer northeastwards to descend a steep slope of grass and short heather, adorned with stag horn lichen. Aim for a broad grassy area south of summit 445m that can be quite boggy on wet days.

Here, keep the high ground to your left and contour under it, aiming for the lower ground southwest of summit 383m just over 1km away. There are traces of a faint path at times, but it is mainly trackless grassy and stony terrain. The rough ground drops steadily around **Q 556**78 **058**78, and here aim northeastwards for a distance of 500m to reach a flat grassy area.

At **Q 560**17 **062**43, it starts to rise again. There is a group of rocks scattered amongst an area of tussocks, compact rush and heather. Keep higher ground to your right and contour along trackless terrain underneath. When you are just under summit 383m, go up a slight rise leading to the northeast of it and arrive at a Red Man marker post at **Q 564**22 **067**49.

Down the valley of legends

Go east for a distance of just over 100m to arrive at a pile of rocks at **Q 565**62 **067**29. Continue straight ahead on the track to reach a cairn about a 100m away. The track becomes stony and rocky initially, then later grassy and boggy, as it zigzags down the mountainside.

There are lovely views down the Anascaul Valley as you descend, and some delightful cascades tumble to your right. You will cross three stone bridges. At the third bridge, two streams spill from the grassy and rocky slopes above, converge, and flow down the valley.

The track becomes drier after this and the valley is flanked by fractured cliffs on either side as you drop down it. The track is initially rocky, but later grassy, as you reach a metal gate with a ladder stile at **Q 574**41 **062**45. In the height of summer, stalks of chamomile, the creeping perennial with fragrant leaves and white-petal daisy flowers, can be seen growing along the sides.

Go through two metal gates, as the stream delightfully twists and turns on your left below the cliffs of Reamore.

Follow the track, with the waters of Lough Anscaul now on your left, back to the car park by the lake.

Loch Thuairín Mhárta and the peaks ranging from Glennahoo to Stradbally Mountain in the distance.

WALK 8: THE FOUR PEAKS OF NORTHERN ANASCAUL

We revisit Anascaul Valley and lake in this walk. The first hour or so is exactly the descent route of Walk 7, but in reverse. Once on the broad plateau, however, we strike boldly across trackless ground to Stradbally Mountain (798m/2,618ft), and from there walk across a line of peaks consisting of Beenoskee (826m/2,710ft), *An Com Bán* (610m/2,001ft) and *Binn an Tuair* (592m/1,942ft). These are the four summits north of Anascaul that provide a bird's-eye view of much of the Dingle Peninsula.

Start/finish: At the parking space near Lough Anscaul at **Q 582**₄₈ **051**₀₉ as in Walk 7.

Distance: 15km/9.3 miles **Total Ascent:** 910m/2,986ft
Walking Time: 5¼ to 6½ hours **Maps:** OSi Sheet 70
Walk Grade: 4

Sunken tower and giant eels

Ascend the Anascaul Valley on the track, passing two gates with the stream on your right and cliffs on both sides. Cross three stone bridges, and zigzag up the track by lovely cascades. This is essentially the descent route of Walk 7.

As you walk up the track, imagine a remote lake in the upper reaches of the valley. No lake exists today, but local tales suggest there was once one here, below the 'black cliffs' of *An Com Dubh*. The lake seemingly had a sunken round tower and giant eels inhabiting its waters.

Just before the col between point 396m and summit 383m, you will arrive at a cairn at **Q 566**₆₃ **066**₈₁. It is worth making a mental note of this spot, as you need to return here later in the day on the journey back.

Stradbally Mountain and Beenoskee

At this point, the mountains you are aiming for rise above to the north and northeast. Stradbally Mountain is at the eastern end of this range,

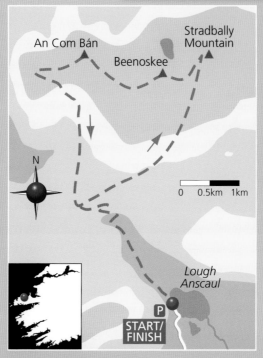

An Com Bán
Beenoskee
Stradbally Mountain

N

0   0.5km   1km

Lough Anscaul

P
START/ FINISH

Looking southeastwards down the Anascaul Valley, flanked by the cliffs of Reamore (left) and Carrigblagher (right).

The view westwards from Stradbally Mountain, with Loch an Choimín *below and Brandon Bay and its mountains beyond.*

and this is your first port of call. Set a northeastwards course across the open mountainside on trackless ground to its summit. The terrain consists of moorland at first but later becomes stony and rocky, and the slopes get steeper as you approach the summit cairn of Stradbally Mountain at **Q587**35 **091**47. *Loch an Choimín* sits in a dark hollow west of Stradbally Mountain, below the sharp eastern edge of Beenoskee.

From the summit, descend the rocky and stony terrain to an equally stony col above *Loch an Choimín*. Then ascend the grassy and stony slope up to the summit cairn of Beenoskee, the 'mountain above the wind', at **Q580**62 **088**80.

Views of most of the mountains of Dingle and of Iveragh may be appreciated from Beenoskee's summit. To the north, the curved arc of Brandon Bay is prominent.

An Com Bán and Binn an Tuair

A steep slope of stones and some grassy patches leads westwards, and then northwestwards, from Beenoskee. You eventually arrive at a broad gap of stones and peat hags. From here, continue northwestwards up a grassy slope to a fence near the summit of *An*

Com Bán, 'the white hollow'. Cross the fence carefully to reach the summit at **Q567**71 **091**92.

Next, descend southwestwards down a grassy slope and some peat hags to a col. A short rise brings you onto the cairnless summit of *Binn an Tuair*, the 'bleached green hill' at **Q 558**50 **089**13.

The entire jagged eastern end of the Brandon range across the Glennahoo and Owenmore valleys may be fully appreciated from here. The view southwest is impressive too: a tooth-shaped line of brown hills arranged one after the other float across the Maghanaboe Valley.

Descend southeastwards from the summit. The rough slope is riddled with peat hags and later becomes covered with more windswept grass. About 1km downhill, you will meet a stream in a slight dip at **Q 566**08 **084**04. Cross the stream and descend southwards on grassy and boggy ground for about 1.6km to reach the cairn at **Q 566**63 **066**81.

Retrace your steps from here to the car park by Lough Anscaul.

Looking across the Glennahoo Valley to the Brandon range beyond from the summit slopes of Binn an Tuair.

WALK 9: A CIRCUIT OF DERRYMORE GLEN

The Slieve Mish mountain range is named after Mis, a Milesian princess who was driven to insanity after her father perished during a battle around 1600 BC. Before the Norman invasion, as many as seven bloody battles were said to have been fought around its mountainous flanks. This walk explores the southernmost depths of Derrymore Glen, deep in the heart of these mountains. It is a stunning amphitheatre: remote valleys that rise and rise again, boulder-filled dens and each time revealing a lake. We take in a horseshoe of peaks: Caherconree (835m/2,740ft), Baurtregaum (851m/2,792ft) and Scragg (657m/2,156ft) on a route that is a world apart from the nearby town of Tralee.

Start/finish: Take the left turn after Derrymore Bridge at **Q 740**50 **110**90 on the N86 from Tralee. Take the right fork soon after and drive on for another 300m until a right bend in the lane. Park here with consideration along the side of the lane at **Q 742**38 **107**68. Should spaces be limited, then park somewhere along the N86 or at Derrymore Strand.

Distance: 11km/6.8 miles ***Total Ascent:*** 930m/3,051ft
Walking Time: 4¼ to 5¼ hours ***Maps:*** OSi Sheet 71
Walk Grade: 4

Derrymore Glen

From the start point at **Q 742**38 **107**68, walk along the lane, following the bend uphill and pass a yellow-walled house on your right. The tarmac gives way to a green road whose sides are flanked with fraughan, fuchsia, gorse and holly trees. The green road bends right and soon there is a metal gate with a stile at **Q 741**72 **106**99. Beyond the stile, a stony track leads uphill and meets the Dingle Way about 300m further. Turn left onto the Dingle Way, follow it for about 200m until it meets a stream with a wooden platform and a yellow marker post at **Q 743**55 **103**84.

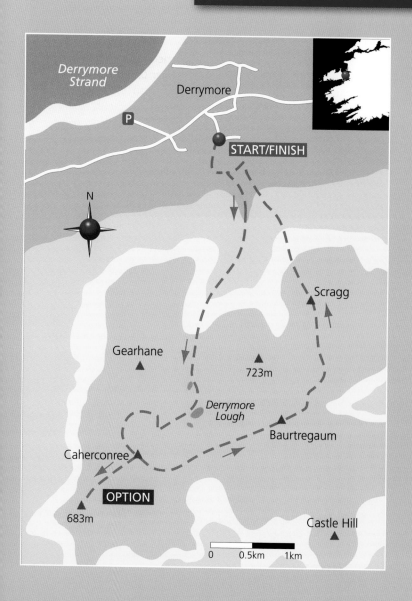

Derrymore Glen

Derrymore Strand

Derrymore

P

START/FINISH

N

Scragg

Gearhane

723m

Derrymore Lough

Baurtregaum

Caherconree

OPTION

683m

Castle Hill

0   0.5km   1km

Mountains and the sea: Looking west along the Dingle Peninsula from the north ridge of Caherconree.

A valley rears up southwards. Pass some ruins; there is also a line of fences further to the left. Follow a grassy and mossy path laced with bracken on its sides, southeastwards initially, but after about 250m it starts to veer southwards as you pass under a rocky crag above on your right at **Q744**83 **102**27. The path is now scattered with stones and rocks as it leads further uphill. A stream flows on the left in a deeply cut ravine. The slope eases somewhat as the towering shapes of Scragg and summit 723m loom ahead of you.

It is now a gradual ascent as cliffs at the end of the valley start to come into view at **Q 744**90 **095**74. A stream tumbles from the col between summit 723m and Scragg above on the left and joins the main Derrymore River. Follow the main river upstream, keeping it on your left, and walk deeper into Derrymore Glen.

Cliff columns above on your right project like a dragon's scales. You are now walking under the scree-covered slopes of Gearhane. The valley ahead soon unfolds. You will pass a drystone-wall enclosure at **Q 740**95 **089**23 by some sparkling cascades. The band of cliffs at the end of the glen appears much larger as you walk towards its end.

A rocky den

You will eventually arrive near a stream at **Q 739**42 **081**33. Follow a stony path to the right of the stream until it forks. Lovely cascades tumble down to the right of a lake snuggling in a rocky niche. Cross the stream on a stony area at the lake and head southeastwards to enter a stunning glacial amphitheatre.

Skirt around the lake's edge, keeping the stream on your left, to reach the ruins of a stone wall at **Q 739**86 **079**94. Walk to the bottom of a jumble of conglomerated boulders ahead. Pick a line southwards up its steep slopes to enter a higher valley where there is another lake. This larger lake is flanked by bands of rock, moody crags and menacing cliffs on its southern corner.

Now veer southwestwards and ascend to yet another higher valley amidst some wild rocky scenery: in places there are conglomerate boulders the size of houses. There is a relatively level area of grass and rock a distance of 500m away at **Q 735**65 **075**02, ideal for a lunch stop. Have a look around and appreciate the surroundings: it is a chaos of boulder-filled dens and glacial erratics. Rock bands and crags guard Caherconree's steep slopes to the west and south. Complex and rocky ground rise to the skyline in the southeast. A steep grassy slope rises up north to meet a spur: this is our next objective.

Ascend boldly northwards by zigzagging up its steep, grassy slope to reach a shoulder at **Q 735**11 **076**86. Here, veer westwards for a final steep ascent to reach the ridge line at **Q 732**74 **077**31. The view now is all-consuming: a string of mountains stretched towards the Atlantic with the Brandon range in the distance and the hills around Anascaul closer to hand. It is an invigorating and intricate blend of cloud and sky, and of land and sea.

Cú Roí mac Dáire

Follow the broad ridge southwards on peaty and stony slopes, as it later swings southeastwards. The summit of Caherconree is marked with a cairn with a small standing stone at **Q733**10 **072**60. Its Irish equivalent is *Cathair Conraoi* or 'stone fort of Cú Roí'. Views down into Derrymore Glen, flanked by Gearhane and Baurtregaum on either end, are good.

An ancient promontory fort is situated down its southwestern flank, near point 683m at **Q 726**25 **066**01. These stone ruins are said to be the mystical abode of Cú Roí mac Dáire, a mythical figure of the

The view northeastwards from the summit of Caherconree: the top of Gearhane (left) is visible, and the townland of Fenit beyond the sea inlet.

Ulster Cycle. Cú Roí kidnapped a woman called Bláthnaid and kept her there. Using magical powers he commanded the stone walls to spin, keeping intruders out. But one day Bláthnaid signalled her lover, Cúchulainn, that the fort's defences were down, by pouring milk into the Finglas River, speckling it white. Cúchulainn and his men burst into the fort and killed Cú Roí. If you wish to descend to these ruins, which are just under 1km away from the summit of Caherconree, bear in mind you are losing 150m of height. This diversion will add on about ¾ to 1 hour to the overall walking time.

Top of the three hollows

Keep to the cliff edge of Caherconree which descends to a narrow, grassy ridge at **Q 737**78 **071**42. The ridge leads northeastwards towards a broad, stony col. Moderate stony slopes with the occasional moss patches and conglomerate rocks rise to a broad summit area which is stony and rocky. A trig point surrounded by a ring cairn at **Q749**86 **076**67 marks the summit of Baurtregaum or *Barr Trí gCom* meaning the 'top of the three hollows'. There are several more cairns around the summit area. Two unnamed hollows lie to its south; however, there are three to the north of Baurtregaum, which perhaps lends meaning to its name. These are Derrymore, which you explored earlier, Derryquay and Curraheen to the northeast.

From the summit, head northeastwards for about 300m until you arrive at a cliff edge. Here, you can peer down into the long, wide hollow of the Curaheen, with some tiny lakes trapped on its barren floor. Follow the cliff edge northeastwards down a slight dip and rise to the stone cairn at summit 819m, a subsidiary top of Baurtregaum, at **Q 755**25 **081**92. Descend northwards from summit 819m; about 100m away you will arrive at a band of rocks at **Q 754**77 **082**32. Veer left here and carefully pick a way down the rock steps and later descend grassy, stony slopes which eventually level to the grassy and mossy summit of Scragg.

From Scragg, descend northwestwards down a steep, rugged spur. The ground is a mix of heather and rocky outcrops, but later it is mainly heather and bracken. There is a faint and intermittent path in places, but this can prove difficult to find in the summer months when the bracken and heather are long.

Just over 1.5km away from the summit of Scragg, having descended the steep, uneven ground, you will arrive at a broad grassy path at **Q 745**63 **102**90. About 200m further on, at **Q 744**94 **104**86, the path turns left by a Yellow Man marker near a gorse bush. Descend the path and cross a metal bridge over the Derrymore River. Turn left after the bridge, and walk by a fence with the river now on your left. The path leads to a gate with a latch at **Q 744**33 **103**81. From here, simply walk along the Dingle Way and later retrace your steps back to the start point.

A glimpse of the Curraheen Valley from the eastern slopes of Baurtregaum.

WALK 10: THE BRINDLED PEAK OF EAGLES HILL

The landscape east of Waterville at the end of the Iveragh Peninsula is a fascinating combination of rugged ochre mountains, delightful blue lakes and verdant green valleys. There is a charm about the place in these redeeming colours of nature. Walks 10 and 11 suggest two routes for the hillwalker wishing to explore this area. The summits of Eagles Hill (549m/1,801ft) and Mullaghbeg (509m/1,670ft) are visited in this walk, but one of the main attractions are stunning high-level views of Lough Currane, a lake nearly 6km / 3.7 miles long.

Start/finish: Take the road east from Waterville south of the Currane River, passing a hotel, and turn along a lane shaded by chestnut and sycamore trees. It winds its way along the long southern shores of Lough Currane, passing hedgerows bedecked with fuchsia blooms, and also birch, hazel and oak trees. There are spaces for several cars at **V 593**23 **651**17 on the left of the road, just over 1km east of Isknagahiny Lough.

Distance: 13km/8 miles ***Total Ascent:*** 600m/1,968ft
Walking Time: 4¼ to 5¼ hours ***Maps:*** OSi Sheet 83
Walk Grade: 3

Eagles Hill

Opposite the parking area, there is a Yellow Man sign, a 'Transforming Ireland' sign and a metal ladder stile. Go over the stile. A stony track leads to another metal ladder stile. Cross this, ignore the perpendicular track and continue uphill on a faint path under the cover of trees. The path is mossy and stony – look out for yellow arrows on the trunk of a tree a short distance away from the stile, which confirm you are heading in the right direction.

Continue on the grassy path following the yellow arrows, until reaching a ladder stile at **V 593**94 **649**47 at the end of a green field. Now follow yellow markers as the path passes a drystone wall and eventually brings you to a wooden stile where views of Eagles Hill start to unfold ahead.

Eagles Hill

Looking southwestwards toward the streaked peak of Eagles Hill from the slopes above Tooreenyduneen.

You will soon arrive at a stream: cross it and continue to follow Yellow Man signs. The path, still grassy, is laden with bracken on both sides. A yellow arrow on a rock at **V 592**88 **643**35 points the required direction of travel. You will soon come to another stream, as the path weaves its way along some boulders and leads to a grassy area.

After a distance of about 500m uphill, you will reach a final stream. Cross this, and continue to follow Yellow Man signposts to the col between Windy Gap and Eagles Hill at **V 586**67 **632**21. As you ascend to the col passing under the rugged hillside on your left, notice the sheer ribs of sandstone rock tumbling down the northern spur of Eagles Hill to your right.

The col is a good place to rest before tackling Eagles Hill. For the keen, an optional hike up to a prominent knoll just east of the col provides good views of the steep profile of Eagles Hill towering above.

From the col, ascend the obvious grassy ramp to the right of a rock rib. There is also a line of fences tumbling down further to the right. The going is steep, but mainly on grass. There is a broken section of fence at **V 585**51 **631**83. Ascend southwards now on a moderately steep grassy slope for a distance of about 100m to reach the spur **V 585**02 **631**39. Once on the spur, veer westwards towards the summit of Eagles Hill at **V 583**18 **630**91, marked by a single quartz rock. The eastern slopes of Mullaghbeg form a proud sweep out to the west, with tiny Coomrooanig Lough below and the massive Lough Currane looming behind its broad dome.

Mullaghbeg and Lough Currane

From the summit, follow a fence line leading southwestwards, keeping it to the right until it turns a corner about 650m away at **V 577**72 **627**54. Continue descending southwestwards, towards another fence that starts at **V 573**85 **624**67. Keep this fence to your left as you descend towards a peaty col. Once at the col, veer northwestwards, over a gradual rise, then drop to a fence corner at **V 562**89 **630**81 where a broad track extends to the left. Do not take this track, but continue on northwestwards, ascending the gradual peaty ground to the 'soft' cairnless summit of Mullaghbeg at **V 559**25 **636**31, where the ground is firmer with grass and short heather.

It is best to walk to the northern rim of the plateau from the summit of Mullaghbeg for a panorama of Lough Currane and Isknagahiny Lough below, and the scratched sandstone slopes of Coomcallee to the northeast. Reed-fringed Lough Currane is one of the most popular sea trout and spring salmon fisheries in Ireland. The sheltered waters of Ballinskelligs Bay, full of migrant sea birds, such as the common eider, common scooter and surf scooters throughout the winter, can also be seen westwards.

Having savoured these wonderful views, descend west-northwest along a broad spur towards another peaty col. About a distance of 200m downhill, you will reach some fences at **V 557**43 **637**42: keep these to your left. Continue to descend the spur until arriving at a fence corner at **V 549**05 **640**69 just below the col. Cross this fence and descend the trackless ground of thick heather, keeping the stream on your right.

Midway down the mainly grassy slope at **V 550**30 **645**79 it relents and there are clumps of boulders. Aim for the following grid location on the descent: **V 549**10 **650**29 – it is roughly north of the previous grid location; from above, a little promontory can be seen jutting out towards the lake near its location. On arrival, there is a concrete pillar at a fence by a rocky outcrop. Cross the fence, and carefully descend a rough patch of bare rock to reach the road.

A walk eastwards of about 5 km on the road leads back to the start point.

The view north from Mullaghbeg, with the eastern end of Lough Currane below.

WALK 11: THE DELIGHTS OF COOMCALLEE

If they say variety is the spice of life, then this is the walk for you: from lake-filled coums northwards to wild scenery above an isolated valley to the east. Two peaks, Coomcallee (650m/2,133ft) and its West Top (675m/2,215ft), are taken in, followed by a descent on a narrow but easy ridge that provides fine views of Lough Currane and Ballinskelligs Bay.

Start/finish: Park at waste ground at **V601**17 **698**35 or by a stone wall at a bend in the lane at **V 602**34 **699**04 east of the townland of Garreiny.

Distance: 12.5km/7.8 miles **Total Ascent:** 720m/2,362ft
Walking Time: 4¼ to 5¼ hours **Maps:** OSi Sheet 83
Walk Grade: 3

Beauty and the beast

From the bend, walk eastwards along the lane for a distance of about 100m. There is a metal gate on the right leading into a field. Go through this gate, and keeping fences to your right, walk uphill for another 100m to a second metal gate at **V 604**52 **699**57. A grassy path with scattered boulders goes steadily uphill by a drystone wall on the right. After a distance of about 800m, the fence intersects, and slightly to its left is a step-stile at **V 612**32 **696**89. Cross this and continue southeastwards up the spur.

The fence soon turns right at a corner, and as you continue to gain height up the heather-clad spur, the surrounding view improves dramatically. It is one of striking beauty: behind you sits Lough Iskanamacteery ('lake of the esk') with its steep cliffs and gully above; to the north-northwest is the larger Cloonaghlin Lough and smaller Lough Namona along with an enchanting array of rolling Iveragh hills in the distance.

Continue uphill on this delightful stretch to **V 619**54 **693**43 where there is an area of small rock slabs. The spur starts to bend uphill to the right. At this stage, leave the spur and contour along

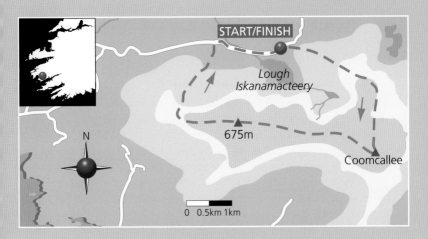

*Ascending the Maghygreenana spur with Lough Iskanamacteery
and Coomcallee West Top behind.*

east-southeastwards, keeping the higher ground on your right, and the chasmic plunge into the rugged glen dominated by Lough Coomeathcun below on your left. Ascend to a flat grassy area at **V 624**24 **691**06. Pause for a moment here, to appreciate the view east towards the rugged ground around Lough Coomcurrane: contorted Old Red Sandstone slabs, scratched as if by witches' claws, ripple like giant waves on the slopes of nameless peaks. Perhaps this is why the area is named after witches or hags, as Coomcallee or *Com Caillí* means 'corrie/hollow of the hag'.

The hidden valley of Coomcallee

From here, contour southwards for a distance of about 300m before descending to the grassy valley below. There are the remains of small ring forts at **V 623**23 **685**53 and continuing southwards you will approach a stream on the left. Cross the stream where it forks, and maintaining progress southwards, continue on uphill for a distance of about 100m to **V 623**56 **683**47. This is a lovely area: the stream with its small cascades and rock pools, the valley with its ambience and remote setting. It makes an ideal lunch spot or a camping site.

After a well-deserved break, keep the stream to the left and ascend the grassy/mossy slope, passing a small waterfall along the way. The terrain now becomes increasingly stony/peaty nearer the summit of Coomcallee, which is at a fence intersection at **V 623**95 **677**31. The view southwards across the Kenmare River and the Beara Peninsula beyond is striking, and so are the peaks of the Iveragh Peninsula to the east.

Of trout and wolves

From the summit, head northwestwards on a broad and grassy ridge. Follow a fence line, keeping it on the left, to summit 642m. From here, swing westwards as the ridge narrows. Just before a col, stop to gaze down the steep corrie to your right, where rocky spurs sweep down to its dark depths, and the edge of Lough Nambrackdarrig ('lake of the red trout') poking out behind some crags to your right.

Pass the col and ascend the slope westwards. There is a horseshoe-shaped stone shelter just above the col at **V 606**58 **681**79. Follow a fence for most of the way up the slope to a stony, peaty plateau where you will meet another fence. Follow this, as the ground drops slightly again to another col. As you near the col, peep down the menacing gully northeastwards – full of rocky crags and a stream that flows down it to Lough Iskanamacteery further below. The gully is locally known as *Eisc na Machtire*, the 'steep path of the wolf'. Cloonaghlin Lough and Lough Namona lie in the distance, with the western tip of Derriana Lough further still.

Keep fences to your left and walk on mossy ground to their intersection at **V 595**17 **683**07 where there is a step-stile. Slightly higher, there is another step-stile leading to a trig point (on the opposite side of the fence) marking the summit of the West Top of Coomcallee at 675m/2,215ft.

Memories to last a lifetime

Leaving the summit, cross the step-stile again and descend the ridge westwards. About 200m lower, the fence intersects, then later turns left at a corner. The heather-clad ridge narrows as you descend, passing some sharp upended rocks. This is a delightful stretch: there are steep drops on both sides of the ridge and fine lingering views, best at sunset, of Lough Currane and Ballinskelligs Bay in the distance.

A fence line soon appears to the left: cross it at **V 583**30 **683**71, avoiding the obvious steeper ground to your left. However, you still have to pick your way down carefully amongst outcrops of boulders and heather to arrive at a fence corner at **V 581**48 **684**26. Cross this fence, and descend to the col east of summit 484m.

At the col, descend northeast through trackless slopes of thick heather for a distance of about 300m until meeting a stony path at **V 581**82 **686**87. Follow this path downhill until you reach a metal gate. Go through this gate and continue on the track until around **V 586**71 **694**49, leaving it as it nears the leftmost tributary of a stream. Cross this and walk between two streams to a metal gate further below at **V 588**61 **696**32. Beyond this gate, there is a gap through the fence on the left. A green path between two fences conveniently leads down to the road at **V 588**44 **700**45.

Once on the road, turn right and walk back for over 1km to the start point at the waste ground or the bend in the lane, giving ample time to reflect on the delights of the day.

WALK 12: HILL OF THE WELLS

Knocknadobar (690m/2,264ft) is a hill of pilgrimage. There is a large cross, called the Canon's Cross, just below its summit to the west. This cross is one of the Stations that line its southwestern slopes and was erected by Canon Brosnan, the parish priest of Cahersiveen in 1855. I have climbed this mountain twice, and on both occasions its upper slopes were shrouded in thick mist.

Start/finish: Park at a lay-by of a lane where there is a single car space at **V 524**99 **874**64, about 3.2km/2 miles away from Kells Beach. There is alternative parking at Kells Beach itself at **V 556**23 **878**83, but this adds a distance of 6.4km/4 miles and 1¾ to 2¼ hours to the total walking time.

Distance: 11km/6.8 miles **Total Ascent:** 750m/2,461ft
Walking Time: 4 to 5 hours **Maps:** OSi Sheet 83
Walk Grade: 3

Above Roads

Walk southwestwards from the lay-by at the start point. Ignore the junction and continue straight ahead until reaching a metal gate. Go through the gate, and you will soon pass a cottage on the left. There are a further two metal gates. After the second metal gate at **V 520**91 **870**67, turn left and ascend the steep hillside above the townland of Roads in a southeasterly direction.

The spur is grassy and coated with thick heather. Views behind across Dingle Bay and towards the Dingle Peninsula are good: for me at least, the last glimpse of anything before I entered a world of grey mist!

You will pass some stone-wall ruins midway up the slopes. These ruins are on a faint path that cuts diagonally across the slopes. It is traditionally known as *Cnoc na mBó* or 'hill of cows' as it was used once for herding cattle from Kells to Cahersiveen during traditional fairs.

Ignoring any diagonal paths, continue on up the spur. It becomes stonier with moss, short heather and some scattered rock later. A small cairn at point 568m at **V 527**34 **862**88 graces the top of the spur.

Knocknadobar

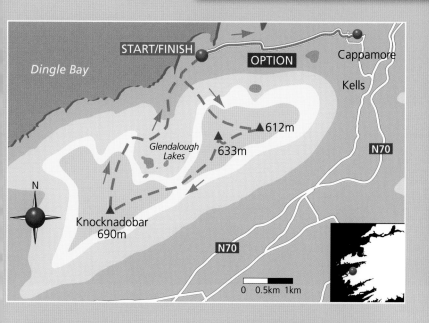

Looking toward the eastern flanks of Knocknadobar from the stone-wall ruins on the slopes above Roads.

Looking across Dingle Bay to the Dingle Peninsula from the slopes above Roads.

From here, head southeastwards to the col between summits 633m and 612m on rough moorland. From the col, a slight rise eastwards leads to a stony area whose summit (612m/2,008ft) is marked by a cairn at **V536**33 **860**31.

Descend back to the col, cross a broad gap, and then ascend the slopes leading to a large, stony area bounded by moss at summit 633m. There is a cairn at **V528**06 **858**26. From here, descend southwestwards on a broad grassy ridge. The ridge is covered in white bog-cotton, purple-pink ling heather and yellow tormentil in the summer. Just before reaching the broad col, there is a line of small upended stones at **V 523**74 **852**13 – a useful marker in the mist.

St Fursey

Walk across the col and then ascend the ridge leading westwards towards Knocknadobar. The ridge narrows in a section above the Glendalough Lakes nestling in a coum far below. You will eventually reach the shoulder where there is a large cairn of rocks at **V 511**77 **846**98. The summit of Knocknadobar is a distance of about 600m on undulating ground southwest. A trig point and a ruined stone shelter marks the summit of Knocknadobar at **V 506**49 **845**16

The Irish for Knocknadobar, *Cnoc na dTobar*, means 'hill of the wells'. There is one such well, at the foot of the mountain near an old pilgrimage route to the southwest in the townland of Killurly: St Fursey's Well, named after the saint who washed his eyes there and was cured of blindness. St Fursey died *c.* 650.

It is now necessary to descend the spur leading northeastwards from the summit of Knocknadobar. The spur is stony and rocky at first, and then becomes steep and heather clad. The Glendalough Lakes are huddled below in a rugged hollow and these come in view about 1.5km away from the summit of Knocknadobar at **V 511**18 **858**89. At this point, come off the spur, descending eastwards down moderate slopes of grass and heather. There is a collection of large boulders about 300m away from the top of the spur at **V 513**82 **858**40. When you reach these boulders, veer northeastwards until reaching a drystone wall at **V 518**12 **862**45. A stream cuts through a small ravine to your right.

Head northwards, keeping the stream to your right until you come to a path at **V 518**07 **866**41. Cross the stone bridge over the stream and follow the path northeastwards, which takes you back to the start point at the lay-by.

The view toward the Dingle Peninsula from the hillside north of Glendalough Lakes.

WALK 13: SPELLBINDING COOMASAHARN

The ice ages have carved out six coums at the back of the sparsely populated valley southwest of Glenbeigh. The largest of these is Coomasaharn, which holds a lake about 2km long. This walk allows the hillwalker to peer down into Coomasaharn and four other coums in the area: some large and others small – but all untamed and rugged. It also takes in three summits, all above 600m/2,000ft: Meenteog (715m/2,346ft), Coomacarrea (772m/2,533ft) and Teermoyle Mountain (760m/2,493ft).

Start/finish: Take the minor road southwestwards from Glenbeigh that leads into Coomasaharn. Near the lake, the road turns a sharp right. There is a track ahead with spaces for several cars on the side of the grassy verge around **V 636**28 **851**37. Alternative parking is also available on waste ground at **V 638**61 **855**45.

Distance: 14km/8.7 miles ***Total Ascent:*** 770m/2,526ft
Walking Time: 4¾ to 6 hours ***Maps:*** OSi Sheet 78 and 83
Walk Grade: 4

Coomnagrossaun and Coomeeneragh

Walk northeastwards away from the lake along the minor road, crossing a concrete bridge over the River Behy. About 250m away from the bridge at **V 642**32 **857**01 turn right, crossing a fence to meet a grassy track bordered by drystone walls. Walk for about 350m down this track until reaching a metal gate. Do not go through this gate but rather turn left uphill on a grassy and mossy slope.

Ascend the gradual slope in a southeasterly direction, admiring the views of the Knocknaman cliffs on your right. About 1km away, there is an area of boulders as you approach a stream on your right.

Cross this stream at **V 648**76 **844**22 and enter an area full of little streams running down the hillside, especially after a wet day. Ascend its boulder-strewn slopes, crossing further streams where necessary, but keeping the general down-flow to your right. There is a stone wall by some outcrops of boulders at **V 646**91 **840**10. Here, you are just

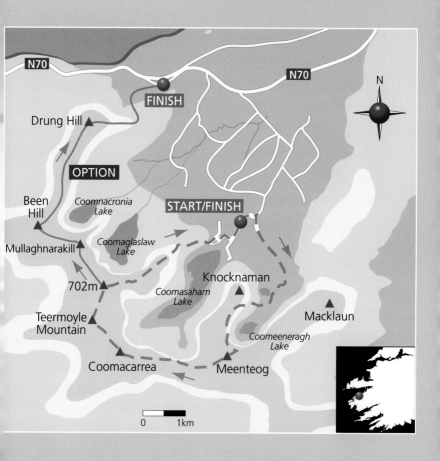

Coomasaharn

Ascending the grassy and rocky spur south of Coomnagrossaun Lake with the broad ridge connecting Beenreagh and Seefin in the background.

below Coomnagrossaun Lake, and the next objective is to ascend the obvious rugged spur south of the lake leading up to Knocknaman's heights. There is a fine, sheltered spot at the bottom of this spur at **V 645**60 **837**40 by some sandstone rock slabs near a stream.

Ascend westwards up the grassy and rocky spur. As you gain height, the lake below comes into sight, as well as the rugged slopes southwards towards Meenteog, and the gentler hillside of Macklaun (607m/1,991ft), Beenreagh (495m/1,624ft) and Seefin (493m/1,617ft) to the east/northeast. During my visit here, I saw a pair of mountain hares scampering up the spur, which becomes grassier as height is gained.

You will eventually reach the top of the spur just south of the summit of Knocknaman (561m/1,841ft), the 'hill of women'. Here, veer southwards to ascend the peaty and stony slopes towards Meenteog. Keep along its rim, as views of Coomeeneragh Lake and its rocky eastern cliffs appear menacingly below.

Coomacullen and religious associations

The terrain becomes grassier as you near a fence at **V 635**74 **827**88, and from here veer southeastwards to gain the summit of Meenteog: a boggy, flat and grassy patch opposite a fence with no cairn at

V63803 **826**64. For a flat summit area, the encircling panoramic views of Dingle, the MacGillycuddy's Reeks, the Iveragh peaks and even the Skelligs more than compensate.

Descend southwestwards from Meenteog to meet a fence at **V 630**99 **822**67, and follow this to reach a rusted metal gate. Go through this and as you near the col, there is another metal gate at **V 625**11 **823**81. There are remnants of an old boundary wall, but at the col, veer northwards to descend slightly and peer over the edge – straight down into the hanging valley of Coomacullen in the abyss below. Coomacullen comes from the Irish *Cum a' Chuilinn*, meaning 'coum of the rolling incline': but from these heights it is more of a plunging hollow! A tiny lake sits its dark depths surrounded by louring cliffs, and a waterway connects it to the larger Coomasaharn Lake below.

Rejoin the col, keep fences to your right and ascend a grassy spur to the summit of Coomacarrea, which is marked by small pile of rocks at **V 611**36 **825**24. Coomacarrea, or *Com an Chaorach* meaning 'hollow of the sheep', is also known locally as *Sagart*, the Irish for

The lake and rugged ground surrounding Coomeeneragh as seen from the edge of the plateau northwest of Meenteog, with the Reeks and a range of Iveragh peaks in the distance.

'priest'. This is interesting as the OSi map marks the sheer cliff on its northern side as Leam-a-Soggarth, which translates as 'priest's leap'. The religious association is also marked by local tradition of a Mass Rock deep in the coum during Penal times where worshippers would gather in secret, perhaps at dusk on a Saturday *(Satharn)*. However, the name Coomasaharn more than likely dates back to ancient times before the Penal era.

From Coomacarrea's summit set a course northwestwards towards the broad col between it and Teermoyle Mountain. Its summit is on an equally broad plateau, so you may have to walk on a bearing to get to its top which is marked by a pile of rock on a patch of peat at **V 603**97 **832**91.

Coomaglaslaw and Coomasaharn

Descend northeastwards from Teermoyle Mountain over broad slopes of peat. There is a fence on a level grassy area at **V 606**20 **841**26, and the spur leading to Coomreagh appears into sight. This is the spur you must descend on.

Looking down into Coomacullen from the col east of Coomacarrea, with Coomasaharn Lake behind, and the mountains of Dingle afar.

There are views of Coomaglaslaw Lake to the north as you descend, but your attention will probably be drawn to the steep grassy drop to the narrow arête, known locally as *Ceimaconaire*, ahead. This is easier than it looks, nevertheless care is needed over this relatively short section. The ridge is a delightful traverse and there are breathtaking views of Coomasaharn's amphitheatre below.

> **Extended variation:** From Teermoyle Mountain, it is possible to continue northwestwards instead of dropping down the *Ceimaconaire* spur; taking in the summits of Mullaghnarakill (665m/2,182ft), Been Hill (651m/2,136ft), Beenmore (660m/2,165ft) and Drung Hill (640m/2,100ft), and passing above Coomaglaslaw and Coomnacronia en route. However, this ideally requires a second car parked to the west of Mountain Stage at around **V 620**00 **887**00. The descent route off Drung Hill is via its eastern spur, veering off northwestwards around **V 614**00 **878**00 and then northeastwards to meet the Kerry Way. The total distance for this variation is 18km/11.2 miles, a total ascent of 1,060m/3,478ft and 6¼ to 7¾ hours' walking time.

At the end of the coum is an area in which locals believe that Ireland's last wolf was pursued and killed by hunters who travelled from as far as Mayo. The waters of Coomasaharn are also said to be inhabited by a unique Irish form of Arctic char, the *Salvelinus fimbriatus* (*fimbriatus* means 'fringed').

The terrain becomes comfortable again around **V 611**66 **841**85. Descend undulating grassy slopes, which later become moderately steep after just over 1km, to a fence at **V 623**74 **850**18. Here, swing eastwards and descend somewhat steeply down the slope of short grass and boulders to reach a dirt track at **V 625**52 **849**97. Turn left down this track to reach a metal gate at **V 631**35 **851**07. Go through this gate, turning left. Here, look out for several rock surfaces decorated with circles, lines and rings: ancient 'Rock Art'.

Continue on for a distance of about 200m, before turning right near some buildings on a stony track that leads down to a tarmac road below. Turn left at the tarmac road and simply follow this back to the start point.

WALK 14: THE THREE HILLS ABOVE DERRYNAGREE

A river flows from the northwest in a knot-like fashion and swirls when it meets the currents of Kenmare River in an estuary south of a village. This is reminiscent of the place-name meaning of its village, Sneem (*An tSnaidhm*, 'the knot'). At the upper reaches of the Sneem River, its many tributaries gush down as delightful mountain streams from rugged heights. This walk explores the high places north of the river, above the townland of Derrynagree, taking in three hills separated by a broad expanse of moorland but offering terrific views of lower coums and distant peaks. These hills are Coomnacronia (636m/2,087ft), Knockmoyle (684m/2,244ft) and Knocknagantee (676m/2,218ft).

Start/finish: At **V 675**16 **706**90 on a minor road northwest of Sneem that follows the twisty course of its namesake river. There is a lay-by opposite a farm building. Park here with consideration and do not block any gates. If it is not possible to park here, there are spaces at a lay-by at **V 672**98 **702**52 for three to four cars (which will add 500m to the walk length).

Distance: 11km/6.8 miles ***Total Ascent:*** 820m/2,690ft
Walking Time: 4 to 5 hours ***Maps:*** OSi Sheet 78
Walk Grade: 3

Coomnacronia

Walk northeastwards uphill on the tarmac for about 300m until reaching a metal gate with a ladder stile at **V 677**61 **708**85, just beyond a bungalow on the left. Go over this stile. You will soon arrive at another metal gate also with a ladder stile. Beyond this stile is a new dwelling and beyond it is a metal gate with a smaller gate on its right. Pass a building on your left, and then arrive at yet another metal gate also with a smaller gate and a brown Fáilte Ireland and National Development Plan signboard at **V 678**97 **709**94. Ascend left and northwards up the grassy slopes beyond this gate, skirting between clumps of rock and gorse patches.

Coomnacronia, Knockmoyle and Knocknagantee

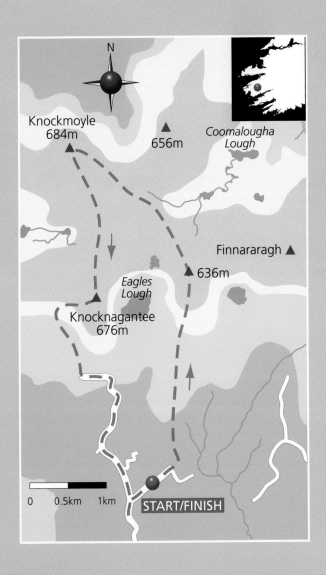

N

Knockmoyle
684m

656m

Coomalougha
Lough

Finnararagh

636m

Eagles
Lough

Knocknagantee
676m

0   0.5km   1km

START/FINISH

Eagles Lough and the sheer east face of Knocknagantee, as seen from Coomnacronia.

Cross a barbed-wire fence carefully after a distance of about 200m uphill. Beyond this and another 500m uphill, the fence intersects at **V 678**67 **716**36. Here, cross the fence that runs down the mountain, then walk about twelve or more double paces following the barbed fence perpendicular to the slope, and cross it at a convenient point. You are now on the open mountain.

Ascend the moderate grassy slopes decorated with bell heather, bog-cotton, butterwort and sphagnum moss. The inviting outlines of Knocknagantee and Coomnacronia loom above as you ascend into the bosom of the mountain. The slope steepens when Eagles Lough comes into sight below on your left, becoming littered with scattered rock, but eases as you near the summit area. A small pile of rock marks the summit of Coomnacronia (*Com na Cróine*, 'hollow of the red cow') at **V 679**92 **733**31.

For the best views, detour about 100m west of the summit to the edge of the plateau to look directly down the impressive coum that holds Eagles Lough and the rocky terrain leading up to the higher valley of Coomanassig (*Com an Easaigh*, 'coum of the waterfall'), holding a smaller lake. On wet days, a spectacular waterfall sprays down into Eagles Lough below. You can also look directly across to the triangular profile of Knocknagantee, the last hill you will ascend on this walk.

Knockmoyle

There is a line of fences about 100m north of the summit. Follow this northwestwards for a distance of another 300m before leaving it at **V 678**64 **736**76. Continue on a northwestwards course, weaving along broad grassy ledges between rock slabs and boulders before descending to a peaty and boggy col. If you care to look northeastwards during the descent, you will catch a glimpse of some lakes trapped on rock shelves, an area we will visit in the next walk.

Just beyond the col to the northwest, some fences intersect at **V 675**23 **742**74 as the ground starts to rise again. Cross the fence on your right, and keep the line of fences now to your left. The terrain is initially boulder strewn, then later boggy and grassy, as the fence intersects twice again before you reach the bald and rounded hill of Knockmoyle at **V 665**11 **749**80, marked by a pile of small rock slabs. There are good views down into Coomura to the east; the wide, barren valley of Maulnabrack below; and the southern corner of the Coomasaharn hills beyond.

Looking at slopes above Coomura from below the summit of Knockmoyle.

Knocknagantee

Cross a fence near the summit and descend southwards for about 300m to a peaty area at **V 665**73 **747**08. Here, start to veer southeastwards to reach close to a stream, which may not be apparent during dry periods, at **V 668**38 **742**15. From here, walk on a southerly course, following a line of fences down a boggy and rocky gap, before it starts to rise again. Continue southwards uphill, passing a ladder stile on your right, just before the beehive cairn that marks the summit of Knocknagantee at **V 667**97 **729**93.

Knocknagantee was one of the three triangulation points on the Iveragh Peninsula for the Ordnance Survey mapping activities of 1825 to 1833, and understandably so. A wonderful panorama of the surrounding peninsulas of Beara and Iveragh beckons. The views of the complex ground towards Coumcallee towards the west and the small

jagged dots of the Skelligs out to sea are also good. In days of yore, locals would claim that groups of people would meet here while out tending sheep. On both accounts, perhaps, the summit is deserving of its name *Cnoc na gCainnte* or 'hill of conversation'.

Walk back to the ladder stile, cross it, and descend roughly westwards down grassy and rocky slopes to meet a distinct track at **V 663**10 **729**51. Follow this track to reach a metal gate at **V 670**63 **715**50. Then follow the road downhill as it passes by some farm buildings. After about 1km further, turn left at the junction at **V 672**80 **705**00 if you parked opposite the initial farm building. If not, carry on along the road to the alternative start point.

The rugged view westwards from the summit of Knocknagantee.

WALK 15: THE CLOON HORSESHOE

This is one of my favourite circuits in Ireland. It is best reserved for a clear day and should be undertaken by experienced hillwalkers only. In the winter, it can be a serious proposition.

Start/finish: At the northeastern end of Cloon Lough at **V 708**94 **788**91 just before the minor road crosses the Owenroe River. You may approach the start point via Beaufort–Lough Acoose from the north or via Moll's Gap–Gearha South–Ballaghbearna Gap from the south. The minor road along Ballaghbearna Gap is a narrow ribbon of road flanked by bare rock, especially at the top of the pass. Either way, allow plenty of time for the drive to the start point.

Distance: 17km/10.6 miles **Total Ascent:** 1,200m/3,773ft
Walking Time: 7 to 8½ hours **Maps:** OSi Sheet 78
Walk Grade: 5

The Matterhorn of Kerry

Cross the bridge over the river and walk along a boreen with Cloon Lough to your right. After a few hundred metres, pass a junction on the left, which leads to a farmhouse. Continue straight ahead and after a further 200m, reach a stream at **V 708**41 **783**90. Leave the boreen and turn left to ascend a grassy, boggy slope in a southeast direction. Keep the stream to your left and soon pass under electricity lines. A huge boulder at **V 713**49 **781**00 is a useful guide in mist. The stream soon peters out after this rock. Another stream, flowing through a narrow ravine, appears on the left further upslope. Continue until reaching a flat area at **V 725**00 **774**00 with cliffs forming a rocky amphitheatre at its far end. Cross the stream with care and veer northeast to ascend a gentle slope until reaching the top of a spur overlooking Eskabehy Lough.

The spur now veers south-southeastwards. You may want to pause to take in the views northeastwards of the MacGillycuddy's Reeks and a range of Iveragh peaks in the distance. Closer at hand, the northern spur of Mullaghanattin also features, rising sharply nearer its summit.

Follow the spine of the spur steeply upwards, outflanking a jumble of boulders at **V 729**44 **775**67 to its right, and at the first opportunity,

The Cloon Horseshoe

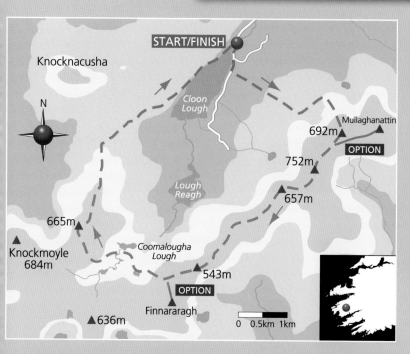

Looking northeast towards the MacGillycuddy's Reeks and Broaghnabinnia from slopes high above Eskabehy Lough.

Mullaghanattin, the 'Matterhorn of Kerry', as seen from summit 692m, a subsidiary top northeast of Beann.

ascend a grassy ramp to regain the spur. Look for St Patrick's cabbage trapped in rocky nooks and crannies as you zigzag up the grassy slope. A stiff pull between rocky outcrops brings you to summit 692m, a subsidiary top of Beann, at **V 730**60 **770**98.

> **Mullaghanattin extension:** From summit 692m, one mountain stands out above the rest. The apex of its monstrous triangular form seems to touch the clouds. The mountain, Mullaghanattin (773m/2,536ft), is known as 'the Matterhorn of Kerry' due to this profile. A there-and-back to its lofty perch can be undertaken by descending steeply to the col due east of summit 692m, and then ascending northeastwards up a steep grassy treadmill to its trig point. On the return, there is no need to climb back up to summit 692m again: simply follow the fence line to reach the col southwest of it. Allow just over an hour for this extension.

The Beann ridge

Descend the grassy ridge southwestwards towards a small col. Next, ascend the slopes beyond, following a fence line on the narrow grassy ridge to summit 752m, a top known locally as Beann. Views along the ridge towards the southwest and down to the valley that holds Cloon

Nestled lakes tucked between fangs of rock above precipitous headwalls at Coolyvrack, south of Lough Reagh.

Lough and Lough Reagh below on your right are good throughout the ridge walk.

Continue southwestwards from here, crossing some fences along the way. After a distance of about 300m at **V 724**58 **761**58, you will reach a fence intersection and the spur branches into two directions. Here, head westwards: cross the fence and follow its line with care (keeping it to your right), down a steep grassy slope towards a col.

The fence intersects at the col. Cross this and ascend another steep grassy slope to gain another subsidiary top of Beann: summit 657m. The summit area is grassy with some rock slabs.

From the summit, head southwestwards along the ridge. At a distance of about 400m at **V 716**31 **756**49, veer left to avoid a hazardous drop down a rocky crag. Pass under a rock rib on your left. Soon after, the ridge undulates on grassy and peaty terrain over points 636m and 619m. It then drops down a grassy gap before rising again amidst some rocky outcrops to a summit area of 570m, flanked by huge slabs of rock.

Journey to the centre of the earth

Next, pick your way along rocky outcrops to point 543m at **V 701**41 **744**00. The following section – the descent into the area where nestled lakes sit – is navigationally challenging, even on a clear day. To assist you at this point, walk on a bearing of 254°, making appropriate adjustments for magnetic variation, for a distance of 700m to **V 694**25 **742**45.

Initially, there are rocky slabs ahead and boulder-strewn ground to the right. Descend carefully from point 543m into a rugged area, following the bearing. The ground rises again soon after. Beyond this, you will be out of the boulder-strewn area. The ground now undulates and is a mix of rough grass and heather until reaching a stream at **V 694**25 **742**45. If you cross the stream you have gone too far.

Finnararagh extension: Near the stream at **V 694**25 **742**45, head southeastwards up rugged slopes for a distance of 500m, to reach the summit of Finnararagh (667m/2,188ft), marked by a small cairn. Allow about 30–40 minutes for this extension.

With the stream now on your left, carefully pick a route down rock slabs and heather-clad ground. After descending a distance of about 400m, you will reach a stream junction at **V 690**97 **744**20 on a level grassy floor. Here, veer left and ascend southwestwards up a slight rise to a lake. The scenery here gives a foretaste of things to come: the lake is tucked into a lonely niche, surrounded by forbidding cliffs. Descend to the northern corner of the lake, and cross the stream flowing away from it.

Keep this stream on your right and follow it northwards. After a distance of around 200m, you will reach a rocky outcrop the size of a house on your left at **V 688**30 **746**07. Outflank this outcrop, and veer northwestwards for about 150m, aiming for a large slab of rock slightly above, ahead at **V 687**40 **747**59. You are now above Coomalougha Lough, and it doesn't get any wilder than this throughout all the mountains of Kerry! The wild landscape here is barren and austere.

Next, head westwards; aiming for the southern end of the stream that feeds the larger lake below from the tiny upper one at **V 685**86 **747**25. Cross this with care, and perhaps notice the purple butterwort and forest-green fir club moss adding a touch of colour to the rocky surroundings in spring. Walk westwards on a rock slab for about 100m until reaching a fence at **V 684**86 **747**57.

Not over till it's over

At present, rocky crags tower above. Ascend a grassy ramp southwestwards with these crags above on your right. A chain of paternoster lakes lie below on your left. Continue for a distance of about 400m, until you are above the last lake in this chain at **V 681**28 **745**22, and the slope above is no longer rocky but grassy. Now face up the grassy incline and ascend the moderate slopes to the grassy summit of Coomura Mountain (666m/2,185ft) at **V 677**24 **751**83. The view down to its coum is impressive, with the steep eastern slopes of Knockmoyle across, and the wide Coombaha Valley below.

Descend the grassy spur leading northeastwards from Coomura Mountain. About 200m away from point 532m, at **V 681**88 **761**29 the ground becomes littered with rock slabs barring your descent.

It is now rough going until you reach the rugged col below. Head northwards, weaving your way between large rock outcrops, picking the line of least resistance (it is easier if you veer slightly to the left). Later, descend a grassy and rocky ramp between some rock slabs to **V 682**57 **764**88. Beyond this, descend steeply below a rock band above to your left to finally arrive at the complex col (elevation: 275m) just above the Glasheenoerreen Stream at **V 682**26 **769**06.

Notice two zinc-roofed buildings on your right: walk in the direction of the lower one, descending the moderately steep boggy ground that is littered with compact rush. Sounds of water gush down from a stream on your left. Cross the stream about 500m away at **V 686**27 **772**25 and reach a wall 100m beyond this at **V 686**91 **773**01 among some gorse bushes. Keep the wall to your left to eventually reach a fence corner about 150m away at **V 687**97 **773**56. Keep the fence to your left and follow the wall. Cross a line of fence soon after and continue to follow the wall, passing a ruined enclosure along the way to finally reach a muddy track at **V 689**75 **774**91.

The track improves upon reaching a metal gate soon after. At **V 691**81 **776**00, the track forks; take the right fork. The track now becomes stony, as you pass another gate and a sheep enclosure. It then bends right and meanders by the expansive waters of Cloon Lough.

There is a small crannóg on the lake – the entire mountain range you walked on earlier rises above Cloon Lough to your right, with the menacing cliffs above Lough Reagh in its furthest reaches.

The going is now easy: simply follow the fine track along the idyllic and expansive waters of Cloon Lough back to the start point on its northeastern end, perhaps under darkening skies after a long but rewarding day.

WALK 16: HIGH-LEVEL CIRCUIT OF THE GEARHAMEEN VALLEY

This is a walk with amazing variety. Getting to the start point may be an experience in itself, as it involves a long drive into the depths of the Black Valley and then into the remote Cummeenduff Glen beyond. The area around Lough Reagh is charming, with its lake, stream and waterfall. The rest of the walk is a circuit around the upper reaches of the Gearhameen Valley, which is surrounded by a horseshoe of peaks ranging from Broaghnabinnia (745m/2,444ft) and Stumpa Duloigh (784m/2,572ft) to Knocknabreeda (569m/1,876ft).

Start/finish: Across a concrete bridge over the Cummeenduff River at **V 821**78 **813**01 where there are spaces for five to six cars on the left.

Distance: 11km/6.8 miles **Total Ascent:** 830m/2,723ft
Walking Time: 4 to 5 hours **Maps:** OSi Sheet 78
Walk Grade: 4

Black is the colour

The Black Valley, with its church, youth hostel and some houses, is almost from another time. Electricity arrived only in 1977, justifying its name somewhat, and the first telephone in 1990. The Irish word, *dubh* or duff, for 'black', is associated with the river, lake, glens and mountain in the area: Black Valley, Cummeenduff River, Cummeenduff Glen, Lough Duff and Stumpa Duloigh.

Access to the Black Valley is either via a long winding road from Moll's Gap or a shorter narrow road through the Gap of Dunloe. Southwest of it is Cummeenduff Glen, a picturesque valley with a distinctly Alpine air.

From the parking space, cross the bridge over the Cummeenduff River and take a right turn down a lane just after it, going through two metal gates. The lane soon forks. Take the left fork and go through another two gates to reach a track. The track meanders around the edge of Lough Reagh. A lovely waterfall can be seen tumbling down from higher ground above the lake.

Gearhameen Valley

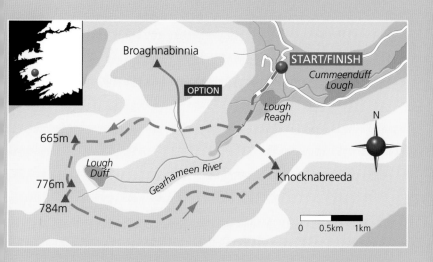

A view into Cummeenduff Glen and its lakes, with Lough Reagh and Brassel Mountain in sight.

The little Garden of Eden

Ascend the boulder-strewn ground leading up to the waterfall by zigzagging along a grassy ramp among some rocky outcrops. This is an area of tumbling boulders, gurgling rock pools, delightful cascades where black feral goats roam amongst the green bracken.

Aim for a grassy ledge at **V 815**56 **804**37, a perfect place to admire the plunge of the waterfall at close quarters. The area is like a 'little Garden of Eden' in the spring and summer: St Patrick's cabbage grows in rock crevices; purple butterwort graces the lichen rock; yellow primroses, purple dog-violets, bog pimpernel and yellow lesser celandine decorate the ground. There are also fabulous views of Lough Reagh, Cummeenduff Glen and Brassel Mountain to the northeast, making it difficult to leave this heavenly place.

But leave you must, and head for the upper valley. Here it is common to see ravens soaring in the skies above. The view by some large rock slabs at **V 814**34 **804**24 down to the three lakes in Cummeenduff Glen is particularly good. At this point, ascend the grassy and rocky ground on a spur leading westwards above the Gearhameen River. After a distance of around 350m, the ground is littered with boulders and there are some stone circles at **V 810**68 **804**48.

The entire route ahead now opens up: a circle of peaks from the ridge south of Broaghnabinnia leading to Stumpa Duloigh and finally swinging southwards over to Knocknabreeda.

Continue westwards onto an area of broken ground. At **V 805**65 **803**32, you will meet a stream running down the slopes of Broaghnabinnia. Cross this stream and ascend a moderate slope of grass and rock, now in a northwesterly direction aiming for the ridge line above.

Broaghnabinnia extension: Upon arriving at the stream at **V 805**65 **803**32, you could opt to climb Broaghnabinnia, the mighty rise to the north. It is a slope with a 345m height gain and a there-and-back distance of 2km. Add about 1 to 1¼ hours for this extension. The summit is a broad, grassy area marked by some fence posts. The Irish *Bruach na binne* means 'edge of the mountain'. It does feel a bit like that, if you care to wander to the northern edge of its broad top, where the views across to the southern end of the MacGillycuddy's Reeks are enticing with Curraghmore Lake

The delightful waterfall at the back of Lough Reagh.

Broaghnabinnia, as seen from the ridge leading to Stumpa Duloigh.

83

sitting under the steep mountainside below. Note that a direct line southwards from Broaghnabinnia's summit to its col at around **V 800**50 **807**00 should be avoided as the ground is too steep and rocky for a guaranteed safe descent. From the summit, it is best to retrace your steps to the earlier stream.

Above Lough Duff

Follow the predominantly grassy ridge westwards, ascending to point 665m. Here, swing left and southwards to walk on the undulating ridge high above Lough Duff until meeting an obvious steep section at **V 787**23 **796**40: a sting in the tail on the ridge. However, there is a worn path leading upwards and it should pose no problems. Upon negotiating this steep section, you will arrive at a plaque at **V 788**07 **795**42 near summit 776m.

The views northwards to the Reeks and Broaghnabinnia are exceptional. The ink-blue waters of Lough Duff dominate the green valley below, and Cummeenduff Glen, its lakes and surrounding mountains can be seen in the distant northeast. From the plaque continue southwestwards for a distance of 200m on easy ground to summit 784m at **V 786**85 **793**72, where a fence intersects at a small pile of rocks. This top is known locally as Stumpa Duloigh or 'stump of the black lake'.

The Stumpa Duloigh ridge with Lough Duff below, and the Reeks beyond, as seen from the ridge leading to Knocknabreeda.

The speckled hill of Knocknabreeda

Follow a fence that runs southeastwards down a grassy ridge. It turns a distinct left just over 1km beyond the summit at **V 796**83 **789**08. Follow its line as it leads down the rugged spur, which is initially steep. This puts you on the broad ridge as it rises, falls and rises again to Knocknabreeda. Leave a line of fences to gain its top at **V 814**72 **792**93 which is marked by a rusted metal post on a pile of rocks.

Views are good to the north and west towards and beyond the wide valley in which the Gearhameen River twists and turns. Stumpa Duloigh in particular, looks impressive, with its steep eastern slopes plummeting down to Lough Duff below.

Follow a line of fences from Knocknabreeda and after about 700m northeastwards, at **V 820**73 **797**46, the fence intersects. The ground ahead rises slightly amongst some rocks. Turn left here and zigzag northwestwards down a steep slope of short grass, scattered rock and splashes of heather. There is a ruined dwelling near the bottom. Aim for the Gearhameen River at around **V 814**37 **803**10. Upon reaching it, cross the river (more like a stream) and pick your way carefully down rock-benches and outcrops to the waterfall at 'the little Garden of Eden' earlier in the walk.

Now it is a matter of simply retracing steps back to the start point in the valley below.

WALK 17: THE HILLS ABOVE MOLL'S GAP

This walk explores four hills west of Moll's Gap: Knocklomena (641m/2,103ft), *Bascadh* (595m/1,952ft), Knocknacappul (639m/2,096ft) and Boughil (631m/ 2,070ft). They are linked by a rugged ridge separated by a broad gap north of Lough Fadda. Also, the descent from Knocklomena down to the gap is steep and on broken ground, and likewise the descent from Boughil to the R568, therefore making this a grade 4 route. However, the panoramic views of mountains west, north and east more than compensate. This route can also be done in reverse, but then you face a final rise in the road up towards the R568.

Start/finish: Parking spaces at a lay-by (**V 851**44 **769**05) above Barfinnihy Lough on the R568 from Moll's Gap.

Distance: 14km/8.7 miles ***Total Ascent:*** 1,050m/3,445ft
Walking Time: 5¼ to 6½ hours ***Maps:*** OSi Sheet 78
Walk Grade: 4

Knocklomena

Head back towards Moll's Gap for about 300m. Turn left on a minor road into the Black Valley. The road winds its way down the slopes north of Boughil. After just over 2km, you arrive at a T-junction at the valley floor.

Take a left at the junction and walk along the minor road just north of the Owenreagh River for a further 3.5km to **V 804**28 **779**34. From here, you should notice a distinct spur rising southwestwards towards Knocklomena. There is a step-stile at the fence just before a knoll. Go over this stile and ascend slopes of heather and rushes, keeping a fence line to your left. Continue southwards for a distance of 150m to reach a track, and soon cross another line of fences ahead.

Keep the fences now to your right and ascend a rugged spur consisting of ling heather, moss and moor grass. Head southwestwards, following a faint path in places. After a distance of around 550m up the spur, you will walk along an area of boulders; one in particular is

Knocklomena, Bascadh, Knocknacappul and Boughil

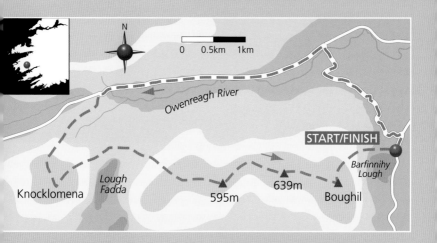

The view northwards from Knocklomena toward the Reeks.

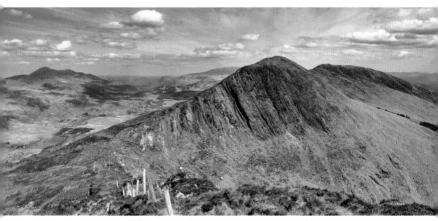

Looking eastward from Bascadh *towards Knocknacappul and the panorama beyond.*

very large. Continue on up, later veering southwards to finally reach the broad top of Knocklomena at **V 797**45 **765**68, marked by a rocky outcrop and a metal post. The panorama of surrounding mountains is magnificent: to the west lie the Beann range and the pap-like profile of Mullaghanattin; Ballaghbearma Gap separates it from Knockaunanattin further east; and the MacGillycuddy's Reeks tower behind the circuit of mountains above the Gearhameen Valley to the north. The edge of Lough Brin, whose waters are said to be inhabited by a 'wurrum' – a half-fish, half-dragon or a half-fish, half-donkey creature – can be seen in the valley below to the northwest.

Bascadh

From the summit of Knocklomena, descend northeastwards down a steep slope of heather, grass and rocky outcrops. Aim for a broad gap at the northern end of Lough Fadda. Both Lough Fadda and the smaller Lough Beg can be clearly seen on the descent route.

There is a rocky band and grassy ledges just above the gap at **V 805**78 **770**82 where care may be required. The gap can be boggy; walk across it to reach a new line of fences at **V 808**78 **771**25.

From here, set a southeasterly course and ascend the rough uneven ground. While you work your way up these slopes, look behind at the menacing east face of Knocklomena thrusting skywards from the waters of Lough Fadda. Pick your way through heather-clad knolls and rocky outcrops to emerge somewhere on the grassy ridge, west of point 591m.

There is a line of fences on the ridge. Keep this to your right, and walk to point 591m and summit 595m, which is known locally as *Bascadh*. The tooth-like profile of Knocknacappul, with its deep clefts that line its western slopes, rises ahead.

Knocknacappul

The ridge ahead is obvious. Staying close to the fence, descend with care down rocky outcrops and grassy ledges: the going is steep but always manageable. You are heading for the col northeast of *Bascadh*. At the col around **V 826**91 **768**54, there is a large, sofa-shaped, grey boulder that you could recline on while having a snack or a snooze.

Keeping the fence line on your right, ascend the bare rock amongst the grassy and short heather, avoiding some bog pools. Look out for St Patrick's cabbage growing in abundance amongst the rock crevices. There is a faint path as you near the summit of Knocknacappul (*Cnoc na gCapall*, 'hill of the horses') at **V 834**05 **767**28, marked by a pile of rocks around a rusted metal post.

The sofa-shaped boulder on the col between Bascadh *and* Knocknacappul.

An amazing view awaits you here, especially on a clear day. One is drawn to the breathtaking panorama from the north to the east: from the Reeks, to the Gap of Dunloe, then of Purple Mountain, Torc Mountain and the Mangerton plateau.

Boughil

Next, descend eastwards down a moderate rough slope of grass and rock to the col beyond. At a point where fences intersect, cross over and follow a new fence, keeping this to your right. The fence intersects again near the top of Boughil, at a pile of rocks at **V 841**94 **764**91. Cross this and walk to the summit.

Boughil comes from the Irish *Buachaill*, meaning 'cowherd' or 'herdsman'.

Step close to the eastern edge of Boughil to be greeted by yet another splendid view. Barfinnihy Lough lies sprawled in the barren valley below. The grey ribbon of road can be seen weaving across the brown-yellow landscape towards Moll's Gap. The rough hillside of Derrygarriff rises beyond Moll's Gap, with the rest of the view in the distance similar to that from Knocknacappul.

Moll Kissane ran a small pub at Moll's Gap when the Killarney–Kenmare road was built in the 1820s. She sold *poitín* there. Its dry, sweet and grainy-flavoured liquid required about seven times its own portion of water to chasten it!

The parking spaces at the start of the walk can also be seen from these heights, and the descent route also inspected.

The descent is rough, steep and uneven: there is much rock to contend with, although it is also grassy in places. Around a distance of 200m north of the summit, you will meet some fences at **V 841**57 **766**68. Follow the line of fences; however, in some places you may need to leave it in order to avoid hazardously steep ground on your right. In essence: pick the safest route that offers the least resistance northeastwards down the slope.

At around **V 846**83 **770**35, veer eastwards, rejoining the fence again and follow its line, keeping it to your right, to the R568. Upon reaching the road, turn right and walk back to the start point.

The view from the summit of Boughil:
Barfinnihy Lough below, Moll's Gap and the
string of hills beyond.

WALK 18: IRELAND'S HIGHEST MOUNTAIN

The MacGillycuddy's Reeks are home to nine of the ten highest summits in Ireland, all of which are over 3,000 feet. It is a range named after the servant or son of Cuddy, a former local landlord. Of all its summits, Carrauntoohil, at 1,040m (3,412ft), is the highest mountain in Ireland. This walk provides two options to scale Carrauntoohil. The first is a horseshoe around Coomloughra that traverses the three highest peaks in Ireland. The second is a route via O'Shea's Gully that takes you along a stunning amphitheatre in the rocky heart of these mountains.

Option A – The Coomloughra Horseshoe

Start/finish: A large car park at the base of the Hydro Road at **V 771**83 **871**17. If this car park overflows, then use a large lay-by just over a kilometre further away on the road toward Lough Acoose at **V 764**00 **865**00.

Distance: 12km/7.5 miles **Total Ascent:** 1,250m/4,101ft
Walking Time: 6 to 7 hours **Maps:** OSi Sheet 78, OSi
MacGillycuddy's Reeks 1:25 000, Harvey's *Superwalker*
MacGillycuddy's Reeks 1:30 000 **Walk Grade:** 5

Special notes: It is recommended to do the horseshoe in a clockwise direction in case of retreat if one does not like the look of the Beenkeragh arête. An alternative route is from the Hydro Road up to Caher, and then to Carrauntoohil and back – leaving out the Beenkeragh arête altogether. Take extra care on the exposed ridge in wet or windy conditions. It is not advisable to attempt the ridge in strong winds or gales. The wind velocity at cols is also higher so take care along sections of the ridge where the path goes over a col. In winter, under snow and ice conditions, this route becomes a serious mountaineering venture requiring the use of crampons and ice-axes.

The Hydro Road

Cross a stile at the rear of the new car park near the Mountain Rescue signboard. A concrete path known as the Hydro Road runs up the

Carrauntoohil

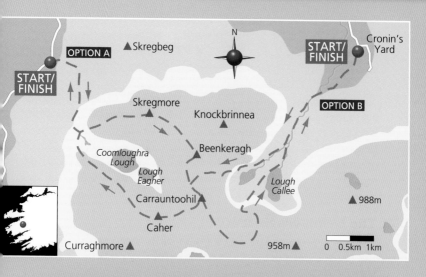

START/
FINISH

OPTION A

▲Skregbeg

N

START/
FINISH

Cronin's
Yard

Skregmore ▲

Knockbrinnea
▲

OPTION B

*Coomloughra
Lough*

Beenkeragh
▲

*Lough
Eagher*

Carrauntoohil ▲

*Lough
Callee*

Caher ▲

▲ 988m

Curraghmore ▲

958m ▲

0   0.5km 1km

*Looking toward Ireland's highest mountains: Carrauntoohil and
Beenkeragh as seen from slopes above Meallis.*

hillside beyond. Underneath, a metre-wide pipe transports water from the lakes above to an electricity generator below. It is a sure-footed way up, but some might feel its construction has scarred the mountainside.

Follow the Hydro Road as it leads up the hill then later veers southwards under the slopes of Breanlee. Cross a bridge over a stream and soon after there is a metal gate as the track veers southeast towards Lough Eighter, the 'lower lake' at **V 777**66 **855**82. The location is an amphitheatre that showcases a view of the entire horseshoe.

A path through slopes of heather ascends quite steeply northeastwards to summit 747m. A band of rock slabs and outcrops guard the summit, which is marked with a cairn. From here, follow the broad crest eastwards, then southeast to the summits of Skregmore (848m/2,782ft), the 'large rocky place', and *Stuaic Bharr na h-Abhann* (851m/2,792ft), the 'stump of the top of the river' respectively. These tops are rocky and stony, both marked with cairns, whereas the cols connecting them are grassy.

The Beenkeragh arête

The rise to the southeast after the next col is a steep ascent over rocks and boulders to the lofty summit of Beenkeragh (1,010m/3,314ft) at **V801**23 **852**44. Its Irish equivalent, *Binn Chaorach*, means 'peak of the sheep'. There are records to show that sheep replaced the goats that used to graze the area after the Famine. Southeastwards, the ground falls away steeply to the yawning hollow of Cummeenoughter and the bristly east ridge leading to *Stumpa an tSaimh*.

A rocky crest leads southwestwards from the summit of Beenkeragh to the ridge linking it with Carrauntoohil. Experienced scramblers may choose to take this exposed line, which later meets up with a path along the ridge at around **V 800**19 **851**05. There is also a faint path to the left just under this crest which eventually leads to the same grid location. However, the feeling of exposure of the plunge towards Cummeenoughter to the left below may not be to everyone's taste.

By far the safest descent from the summit of Beenkeragh is via a prominent, less-exposed path southwestwards, to the right and just under its rocky crest on the Coomloughra (western) side. In thick mist, this path is on a bearing of 234° (make appropriate adjustments for magnetic variation). As you descend the steep path, the Coomloughra lakes can be seen below initially, with the rocky crest now just above

The Beenkeragh arête leading to Carrauntoohil.

you to the left. The path soon turns a corner at around **V 800**87 **852**26, after which there are some short rocky and boulder-strewn sections to negotiate, before it finally drops steeply to the ridge at **V 800**19 **851**05.

Here, you can afford some respite: a prominent path skirts to the right of a block of rock on the Coomloughra side and heads in a general southerly direction. About 100m away, the path approaches a large rock slab and rises slightly to the right of it at around **V 800**01 **849**67. Keep following this distinct path as it undulates along the ridge, bypassing more rock slabs on the way, before finally arriving at a notch in the ridge at **V 800**68 **846**53.

A sharp rib of rock looms ahead and above: this is an airy top of the ridge marked as summit 959m on OSi maps, or known locally as The Bone. Very experienced scramblers may wish to include this summit, before negotiating a way down steep rocks to the right of it and down (southwards) to the col below.

The safest option for walkers, however, is to keep on the narrow path that skirts to the left and under this rocky rib on the eastern side (that facing Carrauntoohil). There is a steep drop (and fine views) towards O'Shea's Gully to the left below. At **V 800**73 **846**38, ignore the faint path rising to the right. Instead, follow the more prominent path down to the left. This rocky path swings to the right soon after around **V 800**79 **846**18, and then around a corner amongst rocky terrain under summit 959m (which is now above you to your right), leading the walker safely to the col below.

The highest point in Ireland

At the col you are on top of O'Shea's Gully. From here, it is a steep ascent southeastwards over more boulders, with St Patrick's cabbage growing in its rocky crevices. You will pass the tops of two gullies, Central Gully and Curved Gully, below on your left before the slope flattens and veers northeastwards to the summit of Carrauntoohil (1,040m/3,412ft). A stone shelter and cross mark the summit at **V 803**67 **844**25. The cross was erected in 1976 to replace a timber cross before it. Its metal surface is charred black due to lightning strikes. Here you are above it all and views are all-encompassing, including most of the peaks in the southwest of Ireland. Most impressive are views towards the Beenkeragh ridge and to the eastern end of the Reeks in the opposite direction.

From Carrauntoohil's summit head south-southwest, aiming towards the ridge linking to Caher. Be careful not to descend southeastwards on the Devil's Ladder route, which heads in a different direction. **Important note:** If you come across a 'Turn Back Now' sign you are heading the wrong way. The sign warns walkers from attempting any descent route down the vertiginous east face of Carrauntoohil where a fall is fatal.

Caher

There is a fine path along the humpback ridge, nowhere near as narrow as Beenkeragh, towards the summit cairn of Caher (1,001m/3,284ft) at **V 792**60 **838**90. There are fine views of the Coomloughra lakes below on your right as you approach the summit. Caher is also a good place to look across Coomloughra and appreciate the serrated edge of Beenkeragh beyond.

A slight descent downhill leads to a stony and grassy gap. Beyond the stone wall and old fence, a rocky slope leads to the summit cairn of Caher's West Top (975m/3,199ft). From here, descend a moderately steep scree slope for a distance of about 500m, after which it eases and the terrain becomes stony and grassy around **V 786**72 **844**21. Just over 1km away, around Lyreboy at **V 777**84 **851**28, come off the spur and descend heathery slopes towards the northwestern end of

The Caher ridge with Lough Eagher, Coomloughra Lough and Lough Eighter below and the Skregmore tops across in the distance.

Lough Eighter below. From here, retrace steps along the Hydro Road back to the start.

Option B – O'Shea's Gully

Start/finish: Cronin's Yard (www.croninsyard.com) at **V 836**65 **873**40.

Distance: 12km/7.5 miles ***Total Ascent:*** 1,000m/3,281ft
Walking Time: 5 to 6 hours ***Maps:*** As per Option A
Walk Grade: 4

Rocky projections

There are a number of plaques on a stone wall opposite the €2 coin-box and house at Cronin's Yard. Walk through a metal gate by a sign that points the way to Carrauntoohil. There are two further metal gates, one with a swinging metal gate on the right. The broad track passes some gorse bushes, hawthorn and holly trees on the left, and then crosses a stream. It then runs along a stony track, passing a patch of spruce and mountain pine on the left.

New metal footbridges have been erected at **V 830**47 **865**86

The new bridge over the Gaddagh River. Carrauntoohil projects skyward in the far left.

and **V 828**70 **864**80 over the stream and the Gaddagh River. After crossing the first metal footbridge, the path forks: take the right fork with a sign pointed for 'Carrauntoohil Mountain'. This path takes you to the bridge over the Gaddagh, after then rises to meet the Lisleibane track. Turn left at this track with the river now on your left.

The track becomes stony as you walk under a small, crumpled fold of serrated rock above on your right – these are the crags of the Hag's Teeth. A larger rocky promontory sits slightly further away – the Large Tooth or *Fiacail Mhór*.

Just before the track crosses the part of the Gaddagh River flowing from Lough Gouragh (*Loch Gabhrach*, 'lake of an area full of sheep') at **V 821**34 **854**93, leave it and veer right to ascend a grassy knoll. There are rocks and boulders scattered on the grassy ground as you pass under the Large Tooth above on the right. Further ahead, the prominent spike of *Stumpa an tSaimh*, 'stump of the sorrel', thrusts skywards: a narrow, rocky ridge leads westwards from its summit to Beenkeragh.

Remain close to the stream until around **V 816**23 **850**62 where a stony path leads uphill. Lough Gouragh now appears beyond the stream, and as height is gained Lough Callee can be seen as well. At **V 813**18 **849**93 the path crosses the stream, which cascades southwards from higher slopes. It is a good place to stop for a snack as Carrauntoohil and its Howling Ridge, the crumpled rock *of Stumpa an tSaimh* and delightful cascades above, the lakes below, and the Reeks ridge all come into view.

Three rock steps, three valleys, three gullies

The path now rises to meet a series of rock steps known as *Na Teanntaí*. The first at **V 812**00 **849**46 is a series of rock ledges leading to a grassy and rocky platform above. The second at **V 811**37 **848**99 is a short scramble up rock steps that lead to a rocky ramp around a corner to the left. The third at **V 810**30 **848**40 is a scramble up some rock slabs and steep grass.

The second of the rock steps – Na Teanntaí – leading to Cummeeneighter.

Once pass *Na Teanntaí*, you will arrive at a wide valley surrounded by rocky cliffs and a jagged ridge above on the right. This is the lower little coum of Cummeeneighter at **V 809**51 **848**41. A cascade can be seen plunging down from a higher valley ahead. A worn path under some crags on the left snakes its way up to the higher valley. Walk to the path at **V 807**08 **847**43 which is scree-filled, keep the cascade to your right, and ascend to the middle little coum of Cummeenlour at **V 805**42 **848**46.

As you round a corner here, O Shea's Gully appears ahead: it is grassier at the top of the gully with scree tumbling to its bottom. There are dark, narrow and steeper gullies to the left of O'Shea's: these are Central Gully and Curved Gully respectively. These were formed due to a geological fault causing a crack in the earth's crust millions of years ago. Carrauntoohil itself is an uplifted fold following an earthquake, but is now a battered stump of its original size after several ice ages.

Follow a path to the left of the cascade to yet another valley – the upper little coum of Cummeenoughter at **V 803**42 **848**32. A sapphire-blue lake, the highest in Ireland, sits here, flanked by the vertiginous cliffs of Carrauntoohil and Beenkeragh. From here, veer southwestwards and ascend the loose rock and scree of O'Shea's Gully at **V 802**20 **846**83. The steep gully is named after Brother O'Shea who died in 1968 after falling there.

Arrive at the top of the col and ascend to the summit cross of Carrauntoohil as per Option A. On a clear day from Carrauntoohil you should be able to make out the path of the Zigzags (the descent route) on slopes below *Cnoc na Toinne*.

The Zigzags

From the summit, follow a well-trodden path that leads southeastwards to the top of the Devil's Ladder at **V 806**87 **836**67. It upper slopes are decorated with sea thrift, whose round-headed flowers glow bright pink in the spring. The slope is on loose rock and scree initially and then becomes stony and grassier later on a broad gap above the Ladder.

Do not go down the Devil's Ladder but instead ascend southeastwards to the grassy top of *Cnoc na Toinne* (845m/2,772ft) at **V811**15 **833**99. Walk on its flat plateau for a distance of about 350m to a small pile of rock at **V 813**89 **834**70 that marks the start of the Zigzags. The Zigzags are a steep path that leads off the slopes of *Cnoc na Toinne* to emerge on the valley floor near the base of the Devil's Ladder gully. From the small rock pile, it heads northeastwards, then north-northwest, before taking a left bend at **V 814**75 **840**83.

Now with the Devil's Ladder ahead of you in the distance, keep on the grassy path to around **V 812**63 **840**21 and here descend westwards (the Ladder is now to your left) for about 200m to meet a path in the valley below.

The Hag's Glen

The path initially follows a stream on the left then later veers away from it. It leads down into the Hag's Glen.

This is where Patrick Weston Joyce, the Irish historian and writer, thought of Carrauntoohil as an 'inverted sickle', perhaps because the distinctive ridges that soar up the mountain's steep face from here resemble the serrated teeth of a saw. Its Irish equivalent in fact is *Corrán Tuathail* or 'Tuathal's sickle', a sickle being a tool with a curved blade for cutting crops. Tuathal was a popular surname in medieval Ireland.

As you walk comfortably on the well-worn path in the solitude of the Hag's Glen think of the poor souls who lived in this rugged valley during the Famine. The glen is also said to be the abode of *An Cailleach*, a powerful Celtic goddess who roams these parts and also the crannies on the Beara Peninsula.

The path crosses the Gaddagh River at **V 821**17 **854**20, where you wandered off earlier in the day towards the Large Tooth.

Now retrace earlier steps towards the two footbridges leading back to Cronin's Yard.

Walkers ascending O'Shea's Gully with Lough Cummeenoughter below.

WALK 19: THE SHARP END OF THE REEKS

The MacGillycuddy's Reeks are also known as *Na Cruacha Dubha*, or 'the black stacks'. One of the summits in the eastern end of the Reeks is called *Cruach Mhór* (932m/3,058ft), meaning 'big stack'. The section of ridge from *Cruach Mhór* over the Big Gun (939m/3,081ft) and to *Cnoc na Péiste* ('Hill of the Serpent') (988m/3,241ft) is harder than that between Carrauntoohil and Beenkeragh – and in places is knife-edge. The descent route is via a spur off *Maolán Buí* (973m/3,192ft) called The Bone, a fine way to end the day, as the view across the Hags Glen towards Carrauntoohil and Beenkeragh is rewarding.

Start/finish: Cronin's Yard (www.croninsyard.com) at **V 836**65 **873**40.

Distance: 9km/5.6 miles ***Total Ascent:*** 980m/3,215ft
Walking Time: 4½ to 5½ hours ***Maps:*** OSi Sheet 78,
OSi *MacGillycuddy's Reeks* 1:25 000, Harvey's *Superwalker*
MacGillycuddy's Reeks 1:30 000
Walk Grade: 5

Note: The summits in this walk are unnamed in the OSi Sheet 78 1:50 000 map

Safety note: If you suffer from vertigo, or are of nervous disposition, then this walk is *not* for you. Do not attempt this route in strong winds or gales. In winter, and under snow and ice conditions, it is a serious mountaineering venture requiring the use of crampons and ice-axes.

Crash landing

There are a number of plaques on a stone wall opposite the €2 coin-box and house at Cronin's Yard. Walk through a metal gate by a sign that points the way to Carrauntoohil. There are two further metal gates, one with a swinging metal gate on the right. The broad track passes some gorse bushes, hawthorn and holly trees on the left, and then crosses a stream. It then runs along a stony track, passing a patch of spruce and mountain pine on the left.

Veer left at **V 830**45 **865**91 before reaching the new bridge

Cruach Mhór and Cnoc na Péiste

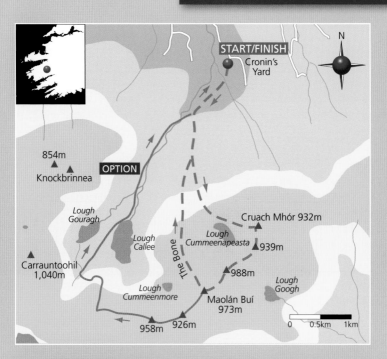

The view eastwards from Carrauntoohil to a section of the Reeks stretching from Cnoc an Chuillinn to Cruach Mhór in the distance.

*On the summit of the Big Gun looking along its section
of ridge toward* **Cruach Mhór.**

at a stream. Keeping the stream on your right, follow the wooden
posts to an aluminium ladder stile about 200m uphill at **V 830**68
86409. From here ascend, southeastwards up a grassy slope towards
Lough Cummeenapeasta above. The slope is scattered with rock and
steepens as you gain height. Views across the Hags Glen towards the
trio of peaks including Carrauntoohil, Beenkeragh and Knockbrinnea
are good.

You might linger upon reaching the dark waters of Lough
Cummeenapeasta, the lake of the 'coum of the serpent', where the
sheer cliffs at its far end stare down in stark silence. Here, early on
17 December 1943, a DC3 transport plane, flying from Morocco to
England and wildly off-course, crashed into the cliffs above Lough
Cummeenapeasta. The conditions were savage at the time and no
one saw the incident. It was not discovered until about a month and
a half later.

Silent prayers

From the shores of Lough Cummeenapeasta, ascend the steep, rocky slope towards *Cruach Mhór* (summit 932m) in an easterly direction. About halfway up the slope, a boulder field stands between you and the summit. Take your time here, using your hands if necessary for balance. There is interesting flora to spot amongst the boulders in spring: hairy cap moss, star moss, wood rush, St Patrick's cabbage and bright-red Devil's Matchsticks (a grey, stalky lichen with bright-red apothecia).

Near the summit, a stony path leads to a large stone grotto on top of *Cruach Mhór* at **V840**77 **848**23. Tommy Sullivan laboured for years to bring cement, gravel and water to these heights to build the grotto in the 1970s.

As you now look towards the narrow ridge leading from *Cruach Mhór* over to the Big Gun perhaps like Tommy it would be wise to say your prayers.

On the edge

At the back of the stone grotto (on the opposite side of its niche) is a path leading southwards to the ridge that connects *Cruach Mhór* to the Big Gun. The going gradually becomes rocky as it descends to a path on a broad section of the ridge about 50m away at **V 840**65 **847**68.

Almost immediately after, the ridge ahead becomes a narrow rocky arête and in several places there are large boulders forming slabs and sharp pinnacles, or *gendarmes*. Very experienced scramblers with a head for heights may wish to crest this ridge. However, it is advisable for most walkers to tackle the ridge using the notes that follow: even so, easy scrambling moves are required in sections and you will need to grip the rock with your hands.

Soon after this broad section, outflank all immediate rock outcrops to its right using vestigial paths under the pinnacles on the Cummeenapeasta (western) side of the ridge. Shortly after, you will encounter a large rocky pinnacle ahead on the left: drop to the right of it using a path below at around **V 840**55 **846**92. Be careful not to lose too much height. As soon as you are directly under the pinnacle, carefully scramble up a short distance to regain the ridge.

This brings you to a notch in the ridge between two pinnacles at **V 840**59 **846**44. Outflank this also to the right, passing a large spear-like rock pointing downwards. Scramble to the left of this projection and then head close to the crest of the rocky ridge, keeping any further pinnacles to the left. At **V 840**61 **846**16, veer right to outflank the remaining large rocky pinnacles before the summit. Look out for a slightly lower path below, and follow this to a rock step which has to be negotiated in order to reach the summit.

If you cannot surmount this rock step, then drop down slightly lower still to about **V 840**51 **845**96 and follow a faint path to about **V 840**39 **845**63. Turn left here to ascend a steep path of scree just to the right of a rocky rib.

Either way, you will eventually reach a path just below the summit of the Big Gun. The final few metres are an obvious rocky scramble to the exposed summit, which you must undertake with care. If you do not like the look of this direct southerly approach, there are faint paths branching off to the right just below the summit, which may offer some easier scrambling lines to it.

A small cairn graces the rocky, elevated, table-sized summit at **V840**68 **845**03. There are stunning views back to *Cruach Mhór*, down to Lough Cummeenapeasta, across to Carrauntoohil and also along the next section of ridge leading to *Cnoc na Péiste*.

It is common to see birds of prey like falcons and kestrels gracing the skies. In the early nineteenth century, a Dublin-born artist, explorer and writer by the name of Isaac Weld was led by local guides to these lofty heights and witnessed a dozen eagles hovering there. Weld stood on the Big Gun's summit on what he and his guides thought was Carrauntoohil at that time.

Weld speaks of the ridge leading to this summit being so narrow that they could 'drop stones into its depths from each hand simultaneously'. Weld then noticed a higher peak ahead, but his guides convinced him otherwise, saying that the knife-edge ridge was impassable. This is where you get the chance to prove Weld's guides wrong. A rocky spur from the Big Gun leads to a grassy gap. Beyond the gap is the knife-edge section of the ridge leading to *Cnoc na Péiste* (narrower even than the Beenkeragh arête). Here you have the choice: on calm days, the more experienced among you might want to try a purist's traverse over its arête. However, others would be glad to know that there is a rocky path outflanking the ridge-top.

One word of warning before you leave the summit of the Big Gun: on misty days, be very careful to take the right spur off its summit – at all costs do not wander down the southeast spur!

Looking through a rocky frame on the narrow arête of Cnoc na Péiste *with the* Big Gun *and* Cruach Mhór *beyond.*

Descend steeply with care southwestwards, down a rocky section that leads to a col at **V 839**82 **843**53. Keep to the Lough Googh (south) side, just under the rocky spur (which should be to your right): this is handy on windy days or should you feel exposed along this section. From the col, ascend a slight rise. When the obvious narrow arête looms ahead just after, keep left along a distinct path.

This path skirts under the sharp crest of *Cnoc na Péiste*, now just above you on the right. You should find yourself on the Lough Googh (southern) side along this path and not on the Cummeenapeasta (northern) side. Follow this path, which is intermittent at times, and occasionally rocky and boulder-strewn in places to around **V 837**21 **842**35, where it veers right and climbs steeply to gain the ridge line.

At the top of the ridge line, follow the straightforward path to the summit of *Cnoc na Péiste*. The view back along its narrowest section towards the Big Gun and *Cruach Mhór* beyond is one of the finest mountain vistas in Ireland. The summit of *Cnoc na Péiste* is merely a pile of rocks at **V 835**89 **841**76.

Down The Bone

All difficulties are over after *Cnoc na Péiste*. Drop down to a grassy gap and stroll along the cushiony ridge to the flat, yellow hill of *Maolán Buí*, also marked by a pile of rock at **V 832**13 **838**14.

Extension: From *Maolán Buí* it is possible to continue on the ridge to *Cnoc an Chuillin*, the 'hill of the rolling incline'. Gentle stony slopes lead down to a grassy ridge, going over summit 926m and then to the cairn of *Cnoc an Chuillin* (958m/3,143ft) at **V823**41 **833**38. Beyond this, a long descent down stony slopes leads to a grassy col, followed by a slight rise to a grassy section. You will then reach the top of the Zigzags at **V 813**89 **834**70. Descend the Zigzags as per the route description in Walk 18 (Option B). For the extension, it adds only about 3km/1.9 miles to the overall route. However, there is an additional 150m/492ft of total height gain. Add about 1 to 1¼ hours to the overall walking time.

Looking towards Carrauntoohil and Beenkeragh from The Bone. Lough Callee and Lough Gouragh sit in the Hag's Glen below.

Descend northwestwards down The Bone: be careful not to tend towards a path that leads to the Hag's Glen. A rusted metal post a distance of about 150m from the summit at **V 831**46 **839**65 confirms your direction. The view westwards is engaging: the moth-like shapes of Lough Callee and Lough Gouragh sitting in the Hag's Glen, below Ireland's highest mountains.

Lower down, the spur splits into two directions. Descend the spur heading northwards at **V 828**51 **844**68. It is a rocky and rugged descent to a grassy broad spur. Cross a stream at **V 828**92 **850**35 lower down. Follow the stream, keeping it to the left. Descend the slopes to at last reach the ladder stile crossed earlier and from there it is a simple trot back to Cronin's Yard.

WALK 20: THE HORSES GLEN, MANGERTON AND THE DEVIL'S PUNCH BOWL

The Mangerton massif is one of the largest areas of desolate mountain wilderness in southwest Ireland. Its southernmost slopes form a broad plateau with miles of brown moorland where herds of deer can frequently be seen wandering. This walk briefly takes us on this plateau to the summit of Mangerton Mountain (843m/2,766ft). However, the main attraction is away from its summit and along its ridge and the edge of its spurs where deep hollows are carved in the steep northern flanks. Here, long-distant views of the MacGillycuddy's Reeks and the mountains of Iveragh are spellbinding, especially on a clear evening when the sun dips down behind those peaks.

Start/finish: Near the end of the road east of Muckross and south of Gortagullane, at parking spaces at **V 983**95 **848**30.

Distance: 9.5km/5.9 miles **Total Ascent:** 760m/2,493ft
Walking Time: 3¾ to 4½ hours **Maps:** OSi Sheet 78
Walk Grade: 3

Special Notes: The walk grade of 3 is given due to the navigation skills required on Mangerton's broad expanse, and the trackless ground to the edge of the spur above Glencappul. Otherwise the walk is on a decent path, and should pose no problems for the beginner hillwalker.

The battlefield

There is a signboard on 'Going Climbing and Country Code' and a sign for 'Mangerton Self Catering Accommodation' near the parking area. A path once used as a pony route for tourists runs uphill from here. Cross a tarmac bridge over the Finoulagh River and go up a stony path littered with gorse and bracken to a metal gate at **V 985**28 **842**02. A river flows in a gorge to the left. The path continues past clumps of bracken and then crosses a stream after a distance of about 150m away. It passes near the site of Tooreencormick Battle Field. In 1262, the McCarthys, the ruling men of South Munster, fought the invading

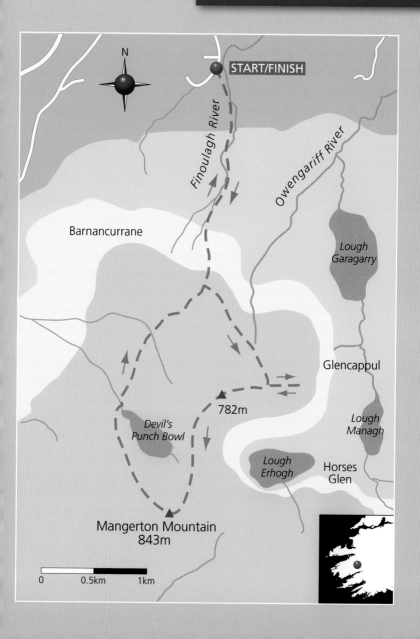

Mangerton Mountain

START/FINISH

Finoulagh River

Owengariff River

Barnancurrane

Lough Garagarry

Glencappul

782m

Devil's Punch Bowl

Lough Managh

Lough Erhogh

Horses Glen

Mangerton Mountain 843m

0   0.5km   1km

Ascending Mangerton's northern slopes with the Devil's Punch Bowl in the background.

Normans in a bloody battle. The Normans were ultimately defeated by the McCarthy's; however, their leader's brother, Cormac McCarthy Reagh, was killed in the attack. Henceforth the area was known as *Tuairín Cormaic*, or the 'little field of Cormac'.

The path, the sides of which are covered by heather, goes up the hillside gradually. A stream tumbles across boulders on right. After a distance of just over 1km uphill, you will pass three rocky cairns. At the third cairn at **V 982**85 **828**11, leave the main path and follow a faint track to the left.

Glencappul and the Horses Glen

Ascend southeastwards up moderate slopes for nearly 1km, aiming for the col east of summit 782m. The faint path almost disappears altogether as you ascend the grassy and heathery slope towards the col. On reaching the col at **V 989**31 **819**28, there is a fenced-off area. Go up a slight rise beyond it to the east, and then drop down to the top of the spur at **V 992**31 **819**68 to stare down at the awesome depths of Glencappul and the Horses Glen below: Lough Erhough in its deepest western reaches, Lough Managh to the east, and both of these surrounded by cliffs flanking the Mangerton massif and the heights of Stoompa. Lough Garagarry guards the entrance to this remote corner further north.

Gold and monsters

Go back up the rise, then down to a col, and finally up westward slopes leading to summit 782m. Descend from here to a grassy and stony track that becomes increasingly rocky. Follow the ridge as it veers southwards, with the steep drop and Lough Erhogh on your left and the Devil's Punch Bowl on your right. As you ascend the slopes to a cairn at the rim of the Mangerton plateau at **V 982**03 **810**64, views down into the Devil's Punch Bowl become more impressive. In days of yore, a monster was said to have been banished by a saint into its watery prison for eternity.

From the cairn, head southwestwards on a grid bearing of 210° (adjust for magnetic variation appropriately) and for a distance of 350m to the summit of Mangerton, taking extra care along the broad plateau in the mist. There is a trig point on the summit at **V 980**32 **807**88

Descent and views

From Mangerton's summit, descend northwestwards for a distance of 600m and a bearing of 316° (adjust for magnetic variation appropriately) to a metal post at **V 976**33 **812**03. Here, with breathtaking views of the distant MacGillycuddy's Reeks, the Iveragh mountains and Lough Leane below, descend the spur northwards. With the Devil's Punch Bowl below on your right, follow the edge of the plateau to reach the mouth of the lake where a stream flows away from it at **V 975**52 **817**28. Cross the stream and follow the stony path which leads you back to the three cairns you encountered earlier in the day.

From here, simply retrace your steps back to the start point.

Enchanting evening light envelops Mangerton's summit ridge above the Horses Glen.

WALK 21: KNOCKOURA AND THE COPPER MINES OF ALLIHIES

This is a simple walk to start off a beginner's exploration of the hills and mountains on the Beara Peninsula. The initial part of the walk gives a foretaste of the Old Red Sandstone rock that erupts like giant bones from the skin of the bog – a distinctive characteristic of the landscape on the peninsula. The walk takes you to the western corner of Beara, to the village of Allihies, on whose rocky hills an active mining community once thrived. Two hills are visited: Knockoura (488m/1,601ft) and Knockgour (481m/1,578ft), both easy and with good all-round views of the western coastline and Beara landscape to the east.

Start/finish: Park along spaces at **V 585**48 **450**37 near St Michael's Church in the village of Allihies.

Distance: 11km/6.8 miles ***Total Ascent:*** 500m/1,640ft
Walking Time: 3½ to 4½ hours ***Maps:*** OSi Sheet 84
Walk Grade: 2

The cliff fields and the copper mines

The Irish for the coastal townland of Allihies is *Na hAilichí*, meaning 'the cliff fields'. The narrow road from Cummeen to the northwest certainly mirrors its place-name meaning as it winds it way through stone-walled fields and menacing crags.

Walk northwards along the road, passing some colourful buildings along the village street, including a B&B, a hostel and some pubs. Turn right at the sign for 'Castletownbere (16km)', and shortly after, turn left on a green road by a Yellow Man signpost at **V 586**34 **453**96. The laneway is decorated with purple-red fuchsia lanterns and yellow gorse. After a distance of about 300m uphill, there is a green stile at **V 588**38 **456**11. Go over this stile, and keep walking until you arrive at a 'Copper Mine' trail sign. Turn left here at **V 591**06 **457**74 to follow the Yellow Man trail as it winds up the hill.

As you walk up the hill it is worth reflecting on the copper mining industry that existed here from the Bronze Age right up to the twentieth century. The industry particularly thrived from 1812 to

Allihies to Knockoura and Knockgour

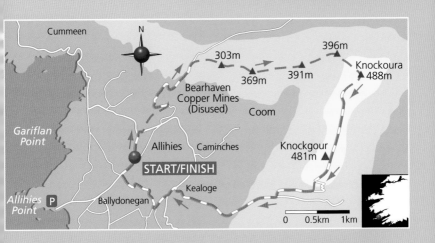

The road southwards to Allihies.

1912 when over 290,000 tons of ore passed through Swansea from these mines. However, this had an impact on the oak woods, as large areas of trees were felled to provide fuel for steam engines used in the mines. An engine house was built on the hillside above the village by Cornish engineers in 1862, which contained a steam-engine-powered device to convey men up and down the mines.

However, the industry suffered after the turn of the century, coupled with the fall in the global price of copper. The area then saw large-scale emigration, and the mine closed and was abandoned.

You may take an optional detour right at **V 588**62 **458**40 for a closer inspection of the abandoned copper mines as far as the fenced-off areas. If not, keep following the Yellow Man uphill. Large grey rocky crags and slabs loom around, as if the inner core of the earth has been belched out from its crust. At the top of the pass, leave the track at **V 594**35 **463**94. Here, strike right and eastwards towards the open mountain.

Knockoura and Knockgour

Avoiding potentially hazardous bog-pools early on, cross a rugged grassy gap carpeted with white bog-cotton. Continue over points 303m, 369m and 391m in an easterly direction on the undulating ridge top. At a distance of about 150m east of point 391m at **V 612**80 **464**61, you will arrive at a Red Man post for Knockoura Mountain.

At point 396m, veer southeastwards, ascending the gentle slopes to finally emerge at Knockoura's trig point at **V 621**21 **462**66 on a stony area by some peat hags. Allihies village can be seen to the southwest below, with Ballydonegan Bay and Garinish Bay a sheet of blue, and the hilly line of Dursey Island further still.

From here, all is easy. A path, which later improves into a track, leads southwards along a broad ridge. Northeastwards, the hills of the Slieve Miskish Mountains roll gently in comparison to the dark giants of the Caha Mountains in the distance. Bullig Bay and Bear Haven separate Castletownbere and Bere Island. North of Bullig Bay sits Dunboy Castle, the former mansion of the Puxleys, who once owned the copper mines. The track leads to some masts at **V 616**32 **450**67 on the summit area of Knockgour.

From Knockgour, a good track leads downhill. After a sharp left bend, there is an electricity pole at **V 613**97 **446**19. Cross the fence here in order to take a short cut down the hillside on grass and compact rush. Follow under electric lines about a distance of 150m down the slope to **V 613**54 **444**74 and you will eventually rejoin the track.

Walk along it until meeting the Beara Way at a T-junction. Here, turn right and follow the signposted Beara Way as it winds back to Allihies village and the start point at St Michael's Church.

The view from Knockoura's western arm: the abandoned copper mines on the bottom right, with Allihies village, Garinish and Dursey Island in the distance.

Looking eastwards to Castletown Bearhaven from Knockgour's summit slopes.

WALK 22: KNOCKNAGREE, LACKAWEE AND MAULIN

This walk serves as an introductory route to the rugged, mountainous region of Beara known as the Caha Mountains. It is only 11km/7 miles in length, but the terrain leading up to Knocknagree (586m/1,923ft) and then to Lackawee (572m/1,877ft) is trackless and rough country – and hence the walk grade of 3. The going is relatively easier across to Maulin (621m/2,037ft) and beyond.

Start/finish: A minor road at **V 718**40 **465**10 leads northwards about 2km/1.2 miles west of Rossmackowen on the R572. Use the OSi map to navigate along a maze of narrow lanes leading uphill to reach a metal gate and finally park at **V 719**90 **483**53.

Distance: 11km/7 miles ***Total Ascent:*** 620m/2,034ft
Walking Time: 3¾ to 4¾ hours ***Maps:*** OSi Sheet 84
Walk Grade: 3

Princess Beara

You are already 210m above sea level at the start of this walk so the fresh mountain air should greet you the moment you step out of your vehicle.

Take a right fork on the track as it contours along the hillside. After a distance of about 500m, take a left at the next fork, in which a sign points to Princess Beara Grave. Legend says that Princess Beara, the daughter of a Castillian king, was brought to these parts by King Eoghan Mór, a second-century king of Munster. Eoghan sailed to the coast of Spain from Bere Island after he had lost a savage war against Con of the Hundred Battles. There he reputedly met and married Princess Beara. Years later, Eoghan returned to the peninsula with an army of men to claim his rightful land, and named the peninsula in honour of his wife.

Further uphill, turn right at the next junction. Walk uphill for about 400m before leaving the track for a sheep's path at **V 721**56 **494**68. There is a rock-slab bridge over a stream, which you must cross. Keep the stream on your right and head uphill on open mountain for a

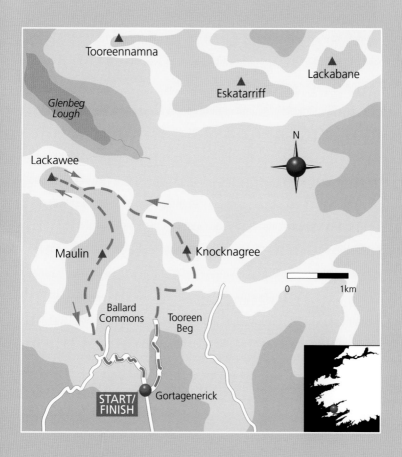

Looking northeastwards from the summit of Knocknagree to Glanmore and its surrounding hills.

distance of about 500m until you reach a fence running eastwards at **V 722**32 **495**89. Follow the fence up rough, steep slopes to a rugged gap at **V 728**40 **500**90.

Fine panoramas

Turn left and ascend the rugged spur northwestwards by picking your way through grassy ledges and rock outcrops. You will eventually reach a sharp outcrop of sandstone rock and a rock pile marking the summit of Knocknagree (*Cnoc na Groí*, 'hill of the stud or cattle') at **V 726**90 **505**79.

You can begin to appreciate the rough landscape from the summit of Knocknagree: to the east, the sprawling bulk of Hungry Hill; to the northeast, Glanmore and its surrounding hills can be seen. We are descending northwestwards from Knocknagree to its rugged col there. Aim for a small tarn at **V 720**35 **511**57 whose western end provides a sheltered spot for lunch below a rocky outcrop. From here, head westwards, dropping to a rough gap and ascending its slopes slightly to meet a stream. Contour along the eastern end of summit 579m on mainly grassy ground and head for the next col between it and Lackawee.

From the col, simply head up the grassy slopes towards the yellow hillside of Lackawee to reach its summit by some rocks and a bog-pool at **V 704**50 **517**67. A fine panorama can be seen to the north, across Kenmare River to the Iveragh Peninsula beyond, with its spine of peaks flowing across its length like a wave.

The rough ground on the eastern slopes of Maulin, with Lackabane poking out in the distance.

Above Castletownbere

Head back down the grassy col and ascend the slopes leading to summit 579m. Follow the broad ridge line as it undulates across more grass and peat to eventually reach the top of Maulin at **V 712**87 **505**32. A small pile of quartz rock on its summit may be difficult to locate in misty conditions.

From Maulin, descend for a distance of 800m southwestwards down a gentle, grassy spur. At **V 709**49 **497**70 veer left down the slope, now descend southeastwards to meet a track a further 1km lower down.

All the while descending the slopes, there are fine views of Bere Island, Bear Haven and Castletownbere to the south below.

Turn left at a track junction at **V 713**92 **487**86 and follow it downhill as it zigzags across the hillside back to the start point.

The view across the Kenmare River from Lackawee's summit to the mountainous spine that extends along the Iveragh Peninsula.

WALK 23: BEGUILED BY HUNGRY HILL

Hungry Hill (682m/2,238ft) is the highest of the Caha Mountains – a rugged, complex and unforgiving mountain range in the Beara Peninsula. This route approaches Hungry Hill from the eastern side, ascending its rocky southeast ridge, and then descending to explore two remote lakes below its dramatic eastern cliffs. Do not let distances in this route fool you: it is as tough as it gets, with plenty of rock, some easy scrambling and lots of intricate navigation. This is a walk best reserved for a clear day.

Start/finish: Take the second right turn coming from Adrigole on the R572. Drive about 2km/1.2 miles westwards on a minor road to **V 780**25 **492**34 where there are off-road spaces for a few cars, or about 100m further at **V 779**04 **493**14 where there is parking for two cars at a small lay-by.

Distance: 8.5km/5.3 miles *Total Ascent:* 680m/2,231ft
Walking Time: 3¼ to 4 hours *Maps:* OSi Sheet 84
Walk Grade: 5

Rocky southeast approach

Go over the wooden ladder stile from the parking spaces at **V 780**25 **492**34. Follow a fence by the dirt track for about 300m until it bends right. A wide valley, with its verdant green pastures, clumps of Scots pine and flame-yellow gorse, appears on the right as you ascend the track.

Follow a stream running down the valley from above, keeping it on your right as you ascend the steep slopes decorated with purple butterwort and yellow tormentil in the springtime. At this stage, be careful not to follow the cascading stream flowing down from Coomarkane Lake, but the one from the slopes of Gortnarea instead. There are revealing views back down the valley, across to Coomgira, and east towards Adrigole Harbour.

Cross the stream higher up the slope and aim for the col northwest of summit 356m where there is a damaged fence and stile

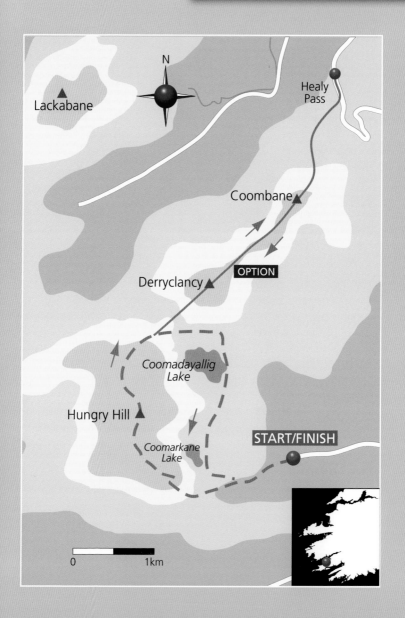

Lackabane

N

Healy
Pass

Coombane

OPTION

Derryclancy

Coomadayallig
Lake

Hungry Hill

Coomarkane
Lake

START/FINISH

0   1km

Looking up the rocky southeast ridge of Hungry Hill

at **V 767**48 **487**89. Above you rises the southeast ridge of Hungry Hill, with its terraces of Old Red Sandstone rippling like waves on the mountainside. These were formed about 280 to 320 million years ago. Face up the spur and boldly ascend northwestwards.

Pick the line of least resistance, weaving around rock ribs and slabs. At a distance of about 400m up the slope (from the damaged fence and stile) there are short crags that hinder progress at **V 764**26 **489**25. Outflank these by veering right, walking under the crags for about 100m to **V 765**13 **489**82 until they become less intimidating. Now face up a moderate rocky incline and walk or scramble (if required) up the rocky ramp to a level area above.

The summit

There are more rocky ramps and ledges to negotiate, so pick your way through these with care to finally arrive at a beehive-shaped cairn at **V 761**30 **492**26. The contrast now is striking: no more rocks to contend with, but merely the soft cushion of a broad grassy plateau down a slight dip and then rising to the summit trig point of Hungry Hill at **V 760**89 **497**37.

There are fine long-distance views: east towards Bantry Bay, south to the Sheep's Head and further still parts of the west Cork coastline with its many islands and inlets. *Cnoc Daod* or Hungry Hill is known by various names: 'the hill of envy', 'tooth hill' and 'angry hill'. It is also the title of a novel by Daphne du Maurier, published in May 1943, a best-seller at the time, which was even adapted into a film in 1947.

A tricky descent

The next objective is to descend just above the col between Hungry Hill and Derryclancy to the northeast. At this stage it is important to note that you must not set a direct course north/northeastwards from the summit of Hungry Hill as there are hazardous rock slabs and cliffs beyond the summit plateau.

The general idea is to walk initially northwestwards from the summit of Hungry Hill, then later veer northeast to walk under some rock slabs, before finally veering eastwards to reach an area just above the col.

In the mist or if in doubt, the following grid locations and bearings may come in useful:

- Walk on a bearing of 352° (adjust for magnetic variation appropriately) and distance of 200m from the summit trig point to **V 760**40 **498**93 and follow red-paint markers on rock.

The view northwards from the summit slopes of Hungry Hill toward Glanmore.

- Walk on a bearing of 316° (adjust for magnetic variation appropriately) and distance of 300m from the previous location to **V 758**52 **501**38.
- The red-paint markers stop about 150m northwards around **V 758**57 **502**58.

Now veer northeastwards, keeping rocky slopes above you on your right, and walk for about 500m, a mix of contouring and descending gradually, to meet a grassy ramp between two rocky ribs at **V 762**19 **506**44. Keep a band of rocky crags on your right, as you now descend eastwards down a grassy slope to an area just above the col.

Remote Lakes

Continue descending eastwards to reach a broad grassy gap at **V 765**48 **507**24 just under the col. Continue eastwards again for another 250m, cross a minor stream, then pick your way through rocky outcrops and grassy ledges to the prow of a band of rock at **V 767**90 **506**88 where there are good views of Coomadayallig Lake below (*note:* it is *not* advisable to descend southwards to the lake from here).

Continue eastwards for another 300m, descending slightly and then contouring to an area just below higher ground ahead. There is a red arrow marked on the rock at **V 770**96 **506**81 to confirm your location. Now instead of rising towards the higher ground ahead, veer right or southwards (keeping the high ground to your left) down rough slopes to the lake below at **V 771**02 **504**47.

Skirt around the eastern edge of Coomadayallig Lake to reach a fence and a green level area. Cross a stream at the lake's outflow and ascend a grassy ramp to higher ground southwards. When you reach the high ground, descend southwards on mainly grassy terrain to reach another lake, the tranquil Coomarkane Lake, in a hollow about 600m away. On a clear day, the edge of the lake can be seen from the high ground.

Cross a stream outflow at the lake's southeastern end, then outflank some massive rock slabs to its right at **V 769**88 **490**49 and descend into the valley below. A stream tumbles down the slopes from Coomarkane Lake to your left as marauding cascades.

Continue to descend with care into the same valley that you ascended earlier in the day. Walk away from the stream lower down in its green depths and retrace your steps back to the start point.

Variation: Hungry Hill can also be approached from the top of the Healy Pass. Although technically easier, it covers a longer distance, taking in the minor summits of Coombane (510m/1,673ft) and Derryclancy (554m/1,818ft), before outflanking the rough ground north of Hungry Hill. There-and-back: total distance of 11km/6.8 miles, total ascent of 670m/2,198ft and approximate walking time 4 to 5 hours (not including stops). Walk Grade: 4

Looking across Coomadayallig Lake to the eastern cliffs of Hungry Hill.

WALK 24: A CIRCUIT OF THE RABACH'S GLEN

Twenty-nine people lived in Cummeengeera in 1841 and only seven in 1871. This is a quiet corner of Beara also known as the Rabach's Glen for reasons which will be explained later. The rugged route covers a horseshoe of peaks stretching from Lackabane (602m/1,975ft), Eskatarriff (600m/1,969ft), Coomacloghane (599m/1,965ft) and Tooth Mountain (590m/1,936ft).

Start/finish: Take the first left turn after Lauragh Post Office on the R571. Continue on the minor road for about 1km, and then turn right, signposted 'Stone Circle and Rabach Way'. Follow this road down the valley to Shronebirrane Stone Circle and to a farm at its end. There are parking spaces there at **V 754**17 **553**32 by a farmhouse. The admission charge was €4 at the time of writing.

Distance: 10km/6.2 miles ***Total Ascent:*** 920m/3,018ft
Walking Time: 4 to 5 hours ***Maps:*** OSi Sheet 84
Walk Grade: 4

Murder in the glen

Go through a metal gate leading into the glen. A Bronze Age stone circle called Shronebirrane sits around the corner.

Walk southwestwards on a green road to arrive at another metal gate with a ladder stile near a stream. Go over the stile, and walk across a wooden bridge over the stream. Head southeastwards for about 300m to the bottom of a gully leading up to the col southwest of summit 406m. There are the ruins of a stone dwelling and wall here at **V 754**91 **548**89. Banks of furrow and peat dug up as old lazy beds for potatoes and grain are also obvious.

A stream can be seen spilling down a V-shaped notch between massive sandstone slabs from the upper reaches of Cummeengeera Glen. This valley above is also known as the Rabach's Glen, named after Cornelius 'Rabach' O'Sullivan who once lived here. 'Rabach' can mean 'violent' or 'vigorous', and this story explains the justification behind the nickname:

Lackabane, Eskatarriff, Coomacloghane and Tooth Mountain

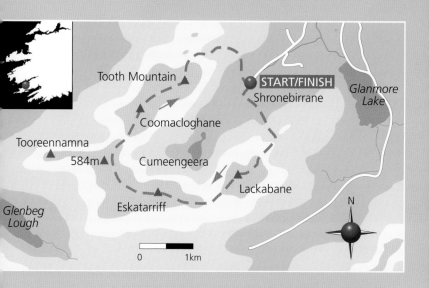

Looking southwestwards into the Rabach's Glen.

Looking down into the Rabach's Glen with Tooth Mountain behind. The descent route by the stream leading to the farmhouse in the valley floor can also be seen.

One stormy night in 1800, a sailor knocked at Rabach's door looking for shelter. However, the greedy Rabach murdered the sailor, thinking he had money on him. Unknown to Rabach, a neighbour witnessed this crime and years later during an argument, she threatened to inform the public of Rabach's savage act. Rabach then ambushed and drowned her in a nearby stream. In 1830, a man fatally injured in the local mines told the authorities that he had seen Rabach murder the woman. Rabach was pursued but each time avoided capture by hiding in a cave deep in the glen. A year later, the dead woman's son tipped off the police that Rabach would be home for the birth of a child. He was captured and hanged in Tralee Gaol in 1831.

The eastern end of the horseshoe

From the ruins, ascend the steep gully to the southeast. Keep the stream to your right as you ascend the grassy and rocky slope laced with green bracken and butterwort. The slope is a stiff climb, and you will be pleased to finally emerge at a grassy col at **V 758**58 **542**82.

The col is a good place to appreciate the wide green valley below, with its ancient field systems and the Drimminboy River cutting a course through it. The sandstone crags that line up at the valley's western end can also be observed, rising as contorted folds to the heights of Tooth Mountain beyond.

From the col, follow the ridge that leads southwest, going up steep grassy slopes and weaving through rock outcrops. There is a small pile of rock at **V 754**94 **538**18 marking the top of Curraghreague. Now the gradient eases. Views of Kilmakilloge Harbour, tucked behind green pastures and rolling brown hills to the north fills the scope of vision, as well as Glanmore valley to the right and the Iveragh Peninsula beyond.

Continue on easy grassy ground to the summit of Lackabane (*An Leaca Bhán*, 'the white hillside') about 400m away at **V 751**44 **536**92. Descend southwestwards from Lackabane, following the cliff edge and picking the safest line down waves of sandstone slabs that seem to guard its slope. There is a grassy strip between two rock ribs that eases the descent somewhat.

Continue to follow the cliff edge and follow it down to a rugged gap. A slight rise now beckons westwards: follow a fence that stops short of summit 531m at **V 742**89 **531**54. The view of the northern ramparts of Hungry Hill across Glanmore are impressive from here.

Cummeengeera Glen as seen from Eskatarriff's summit slopes: Tooth Mountain rises on the left, while Lackabane is the pointed peak on the right.

From summit 531m, still keeping to the cliff edge, ascend moderate slopes to arrive at the grassy summit of Eskatarriff at **V 736**48 **533**25.

You are now standing on the Cork–Kerry border. One of the gullies on its northern ramparts, often in shadow, is known as *Eisc a' Tairbh* or the 'steep path of the bull'. The dark presence of the Hag of Beara, also known as *Boí or Buí*, which comes from the old word for 'cow', is said to haunt these steep crannies according to folklore. The Hag herself is a powerful, ancient Celtic goddess of the sea, of creation, of death and a protector of the wild. Views of the entire Cummeengeera Valley below and both arms of the horseshoe – Coomacloghane and Tooth Mountain on the left and Lackabane on the right – are exceptional.

The western end of the horseshoe

From Eskatarriff, meander westwards across a broad, grassy and peaty gap. A slight rise leads to a small pile of stones on a rocky

The view southeastwards from the summit of Coomacloghane: the sprawling mass of Hungry Hill can be seen in the distance.

outcrop that marks summit 596m at **V 730**76 **534**01. From here, veer northwestwards. A gradual descent leads to summit 584m. However, there is no need to go there, but rather contour to the right and descend to a peaty gap.

You are now on the opposite end of the horseshoe and a slope now rises to the northeast. Keep to the right of the slope and ascend its rugged, rocky line to the trig point of Coomacloghane (*Com an Chlocháin*, 'coum of the stone dwelling'), perched on an outcrop of rock at **V 732**63 **548**16. If you arrive here in late afternoon, the mountains on the opposite end should be bathed in evening light, hence justifying doing the horseshoe in this direction.

From Coomacloghane, descend northeastwards to a gap and arrive at a fence corner at **V 738**36 **552**66 as the cliff edge veers eastwards. You now need to head in that direction to arrive at some rock outcrops at **V 741**85 **553**17 on the summit of Tooth Mountain. Descend northwards from this summit for about 100m to meet a fence line at **V 741**47 **554**31. Follow this line, keeping it to your right, to a rugged gap.

Steep descent

At the lowest point of the gap (**V 742**37 **557**99), cross the fence line and descend the ground to your right. It is a steep gully composed of short grass, heather and rocks. Follow a stream, keeping it to your right. Further down, the slope is less steep along a grassy stretch but later as the stream veers southwards, it gets steep again.

Walk through bracken (which can be thick in the summer) lower down the steep slopes to reach a fence and cross it with care at its corner (**V 752**37 **556**11). Cross the stream beyond the fence. Descend the gentle slopes to reach a stone-wall ruin and eventually a metal gate at **V 752**14 **554**33.

Follow the track and go through another gate to reach a lane that leads back to the farmhouse.

WALK 25: A CONNOISSEUR'S ROUTE OF KNOCKOWEN

Knockowen or 'the hill of Owen' rises to 658m/2,159ft in the heart of the Caha Mountains and above the Healy Pass. Being the highest point in the Cahas east of this Pass, and second in height only to Hungry Hill, its summit boasts far-reaching views of Beara and Iveragh. Although a direct ascent from the Pass is possible, this unique route takes us on the tongue-twisting minor summit of Stookeennalaokareha (412m/1,352ft) for glorious views down into Glanmore, and a peek into the jaw-dropping Glanrastel valley. Knockowen itself is then surmounted, followed by the rugged hill of Cushnaficulla (594m/1,949ft), before descending under Knockowen's impressive southern ramparts, guarded by massive sandstone slabs. It's a connoisseur's route of the area!

Start/finish: Parking area at **V 785**33 **538**77, located about 800m after a severe V-bend near the top of Healy Pass.

Distance: 9km/5.6 miles **Total Ascent:** 600m/1,968ft
Walking Time: 3¼ to 4 hours **Maps:** OSi Sheet 84
Walk Grade: 4

The Healy Pass and Stookeennalaokareha

It may be difficult to even get going, as the views from the parking area into the Glanmore Valley are exceptionally good. But at least it is downhill to begin with, so walk back down the Healy Pass road to the V-bend at **V 790**13 **545**39 where a wide stream flows under an arched bridge. The road was named after Tim Healy, the first Governor General of the Irish Free State from 1922 to 1927, who was originally from nearby Bantry.

While walking down the road, you may not even notice the mountainside on the east, as the eye is constantly drawn to the blue waters of Glanmore Lake in the elongated valley below you to the left, and to the mountains that rise commandingly above its yellow-green plains. This view towards the lake gets better and better as you ascend the grassy slopes scattered with boulders to three small knolls that mark Stookeennalaokareha's summit area at **V 792**32 **550**79.

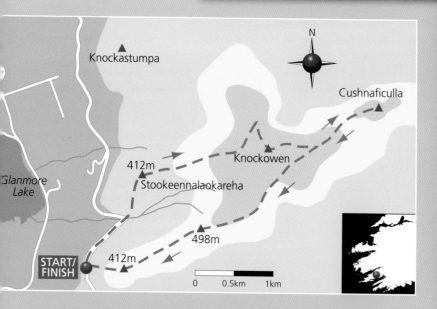

A stunning view of Glanmore Lake and the mountains of the Rabach's Glen, as seen from the summit of Stookeennalaokareha.

Here, pause for a moment to take it all in: the grey ribbon of road below; the spur running southwest over Coombane, Derryclancy and Hungry Hill; extended views into Glanmore Valley and the hills beyond; Glanmore Lake and the mountains of the Rabach's Glen that rise behind it; and the hills of the Iveragh Peninsula in the distance.

Glanrastel and Knockowen

Continue on uphill along the green undulating spur sprinkled with rocks, and then contour northeast at around **V 804**00 **553**50 to head for the col at **V 806**94 **557**60, between Knockowen and a minor rise. Glanrastel is a wide, rugged valley in the depths below, framed by sheer sandstone cliffs. Its river and its many tributaries can be seen twisting along the valley floor and also snaking down the rough hillside beyond from the heights of Cummeenbaun and Droppa.

The next stage of the walk leads southeast over rocky terrain to the summit of Knockowen at **V 808**68 **553**94, whose highest point is a cairn perched on a rib of rock. This hill is attributed to a man named Owen, or Eoghan, and his legacy lives on around Beara in place names such as Kilmackowen and Rossmackowen. Folklore points to a second century King of Munster by the name of *Eoghan Mór*, who sailed to Spain from Bere Island after he lost a fight against Con of the Hundred Battles, a Connacht High King. Views of distant Iveragh peaks are good and a range of rugged Beara Hills can also be seen westwards, including Hungry Hill. To the northeast there is the stark landscape of bog and rock leading to the summit of Cushnaficulla, our next objective.

Cushnaficulla

Descend Knockowen, initially eastwards down the rugged spur, negotiating slabs and ribs of sandstone rock, and then later swinging northeast towards a grassy col, where there is a small tarn at **V 817**86 **557**51. From the tarn, ascend a moderate slope for about 350m to a small rock pile sitting on a larger piece of rock that marks the summit of Cushnaficulla at **V 821**34 **559**26. Views of the distant Iveragh Peninsula from here are even better than those from Knockowen. The sweeping profile of Knockowen's steep, striated northern cliffs catches the eye, and also the rugged landscape of the Caha lakes to the northeast.

Note: In mist and/or rain, instead of progression to Cushnaficulla, you may choose a more direct route down the southwest spur of Knockowen and over Claddaghgarriff. This leads back to the start/ finish point on the Healy Pass.

The distant view of the Iveragh Peninsula and its spine of mountains from the summit of Cushnaficulla.

A tricky descent

From Cushnaficulla's summit, retrace steps back down to the small tarn on the col, and ascend the spur beyond it for a distance of about 500m to **V 814**02 **554**65, where there is a distinct upended boulder perched on a rocky outcrop. There are large rock slabs above ahead. At this point, veer left under massive sandstone slabs above and descend in a general southwesterly direction towards the top of a valley.

At **V 809**35 **550**43, resist the urge to drop into this valley but rather contour above it on grassy ground under some large and diagonally slanting rock slabs on your right. The wide upper Kilcaskan Valley is on your left as you initially pass under Knockowen's monstrous southern slabs. Contour along southwestwards, with high ground on your right, and in the mist take care not to descend the southern spur above the Clashduff River.

The terrain becomes slightly rocky at **V 801**54 **544**11 and here turn right and walk a short distance uphill along a broad grassy ramp between rocky outcrops to the top of the Claddaghgarriff spur at **V 800**80 **544**78. Once on this spur simply follow its line, initially going up a slight rise and then walking on undulating grassy and rocky terrain, until reaching a hive-shaped cairn at **V 792**36 **540**09. Continue to descend the spur, picking your way down grassy ledges amongst rocky outcrops to reach a metal pipe bolted into the rock at **V 789**21 **539**05.

From here, walk due west for about 100m, and while standing atop a large rock slab, you should see your car parked at the start point of the walk. Simply walk down the slope – decorated with butterwort and tormentil in spring – back to your car.

WALK 26: AN EXTENDED CIRCUIT OF GLANINCHIQUIN

Glaninchiquin is a lonely and idyllic valley at the end of a minor country lane leading southeast between the Killaha and Tuosist roads on the R571. There are lovely lakes south of this lane. A horseshoe of hills surrounds its largest lake, Lough Inchiquin. This walk explores all these hills above its glacial valley: Knockagarrane (414m/1,358ft), Knockreagh (500m/1,640ft), Coomnadiha (644m/2,113ft), Knocknagorraveela (507m/1,663ft) and Derrysallagh (410m/1,345ft). It is a full-day walk in typically rough and rugged Caha terrain, but one that rewards the hillwalker with some remarkable views.

Start/finish: Park at a lay-by near a junction between Cloonee Lough Upper and Lough Inchiquin at **V 830**75 **638**51 where there are spaces for several cars.

Distance: 20km/12.4 miles ***Total Ascent:*** 1,050m/3,445ft
Walking Time: 6¾ to 8½ hours ***Maps:*** OSi Sheet 84 and 85
Walk Grade: 4

Special notes: The terrain between Coomnadiha and point 435m (**V 862**50 **602**00) is especially rough.

Knockgarrane

Walk southwest along the Beara Way. There is a metal gate at the bridge over the Ameen River. Slightly further, you will pass a sign for a stone circle with a metal coin box on the left. Enormous rushes grow by the lane, and there is another metal gate soon after. Go through this gate, passing a sheep pen before the lane skirts uphill. There is a sign for a Famine house, then a boulder burial. A broad track bends right and uphill to a new cottage at its end at **V 823**08 **632**51. Here bear right, following a Yellow Man sign and going through two metal gates. The Yellow Man signs lead uphill through patches of yellow gorse.

Walk up moderately grassy, butterwort-covered slopes to the top of a pass at **V 818**75 **627**14. Cross a fence and then pick your way along grassy benches amongst the rock slabs that guard the northern slopes of Knockagarrane. You will eventually reach the summit at point

Glaninchiquin

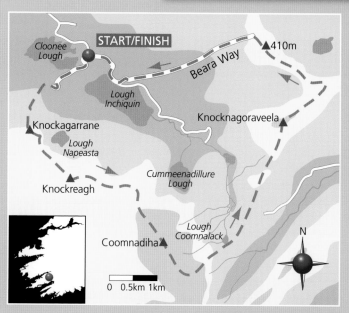

Looking northeast down to Cummeenadillure Lough, and the glacial valley of Glaninchiquin from the col between Cummeenanimma and Coumnadiha.

414m on the map, but walk on to **V 820**59 **622**59 for the best views of Lough Inchiquin, nearly 1.5km long, and Cloonee Lough Upper in the valley below.

Robbers, a boot of gold and an eagle's nest

The descent southwards to the col above Lough Napeasta is rugged: it is best to follow a fence line at around **V 820**30 **621**36, and then outflank a rocky outcrop on the left, picking your way carefully along a series of grassy ramps down to the col. From the col, ascend a moderate slope southeast, crossing fences where necessary, until reaching the top of Knockreagh at **V826**98 **613**55.

From here walk just south of Lough Naneeslee, and follow a line of fences towards a broad and grassy col. Cross a new fence at **V 840**92 **613**47: at this stage you must decide whether or not to walk a short distance of 300m downhill to the edge of the Cummeenanimma spur (**V 842**59 **614**18) for the best views into Glaninchiquin below. To the left of the spur is an area known locally as the Robber's Den. It is said that an outlaw dropped a 'golden boot' in the river below during a pursuit that resulted in his being shot near the hills of Bunane, further east. The lake to the right of the spur is Cummeenadillure Lough, where an eagle's nest once sat in the steep ground above it. The view northwest is the best, down into the rugged glacial valley of Glaninchiquin, with a waterfall plunging down to its valley floor at the end of it.

If not on the detour to the edge of Cummeenanimma, then head south from **V 840**92 **613**47, crossing a rugged gap with peat hags, and later veering southeast to ascend grassy and rocky terrain leading to the summit trig point of Coomnadiha at **V 847**30 **600**38.

A taste of Caha sandstone

Leaving the summit, descend southeastwards on a grassy patch, followed by a slight rise to a peaty area around point 613m. About 100m away from this point at **V 852**88 **594**26, there is a large flat rock with some smaller rocks on top. Veer left here, descending down a spur to an obvious narrow, grassy strip between two very large and long ribs of rock at **V 853**55 **595**30 (the grid location could be useful in the mist, as the ground is rough). These rock ribs and slabs run down the rugged spur to an equally rugged gap. These sandstone slabs run riot like rocky waves, only to subside again into a brown sea of bog.

It is all rough going, typical of the Cahas. Once at the gap, pick a path to the right of some rocky outcrops. A stunning and remote valley, the Baurearagh, opens up to the right. (More of this delightful valley is explored in Walk 27.) The Old Red Sandstone rock that makes up terra firma is streaked with quartz. The sharp-pointed green shoots of fir clubmoss and the violet, dual-lipped, single flowers of butterwort

The rugged ridge east of Coumnadiha, with Lough Coomnalack just below and Knocknagorraveela beyond.

Glaninchiquin, as seen from the quiet valley north of Knocknagorraveela, late on a spring evening.

also grace the area.

Knocknagorraveela and Derrysallagh

A lake, Lough Coomnalack, tucked into a rugged corner, appears below on the left. Do not descend into it, but rather ascend the spur northeastwards to point 435m. From here, descend on grass and bare rock to a fence at **V 864**56 **605**95. During the descent, you will notice a green-roofed hut by a clump of trees on slopes above the Baurearagh Valley below you to the right, an almost surreal sight amidst such a wild setting. Follow this fence northeastwards up a gentle slope to **V 867**46 **613**10 where the fence swings right. At this point, leave the fence, and continue northeastwards along moorland until reaching the summit of Knocknagorraveela at **V 871**35 **624**95, known in Irish as *Cnoc na gCorra-mhíola* or the 'hill of midges'. However, there were none in sight during my visit.

From here, continue northeastwards to point 464m (**V 881**00 **633**00) and then veer northwestwards to the minor summit of Derrysallagh (**V 867**00 **640**50) on broad ridges. Leaving Derrysallagh, descend northwestwards for a distance of 300m, and you will meet the Beara Way at around **V 865**00 **642**20. Simply follow the waymarked route down the hill, then later on tarmac until reaching a junction at **V 836**50 **633**00. Turn right at the junction, and this will take you back to the start point.

Gleninchaquin Park: Although it is marked on the OSi map as Glaninchiquin, the park at the end of the valley is advertised as *'Gleninchaquin'* on www.gleninchaquin.com. The park provides parking facilities, picnic tables, home baking, teas and coffee refreshments. Activities include walking (details of all the walks are available on the website provided – and all of them are easier than this one if you fancy a shorter day), fishing, bird-watching, botany, a working farm and a heritage site. At the time of writing, admission charges were €5 for adults, €3.00 for students, with free entry for children under twelve.

The waterfall at the end of Glaninchiquin, near its park and farm.

WALK 27: THE VALLEY THAT TIME FORGOT

A long, narrow and lonely road leads southwestwards from near Releagh Bridge on the N71. It winds its way north of the Baurearagh River, charting a course into a remote green valley of the same name. It is a quiet corner of Beara, where one can almost hear the breeze whispering gently against the moor grass. I love the peacefulness of this place – long may it remain untouched and unchanged by the hands of modern progress! This walk explores the best of the area, initially along the valley floor, then ascending a spur to the broad plateau of Caha (608m/1,995ft) and finally traversing a narrow grassy ridge, taking in Killane Mountain (537m/1,762ft) and Baurearagh Mountain (489m/1,604ft) along the way.

Start/finish: There is a single parking space on a grassy verge at **V 880**25 **615**70, just before a narrow lane that heads southwards down the Baurearagh Valley. If you cannot park here, backtrack 800m along the road to **V 888**14 **617**12 where there are ample parking spaces.

Distance: 10.5km/6.5 miles ***Total Ascent:*** 650m/2,133ft
Walking Time: 3¾ to 4½ hours ***Maps:*** OSi Sheet 85
Walk Grade: 4

Stepping away from civilisation

From the road, take the immediate left down the lane with a postbox by a metal gate. Go through another metal gate just before the bridge over a stream, pass a cottage on the right with a garage on its left, followed by yet another metal gate before reaching a junction.

Turn right at this junction and walk through a metal gate. This will take you along a lane whose sides are adorned with rhododendron and gorse. There is also a clump of Scots pine nearby and some conifers in the valley further to your right.

The lane passes a zinc-roofed workhouse and deserted bungalow on the right. Continue on, walk through two metal gates and then along a green road, passing through another two metal gates shortly

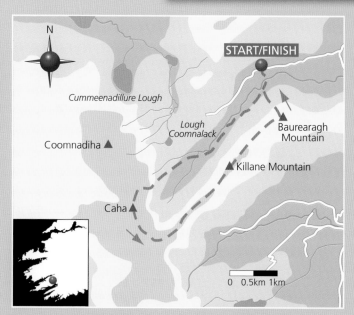

Caha, Killane and Baurearagh

Looking southwest into the remote Baurearagh Valley, flanked by Killane Mountain on the left and the cliffs of Caha at its end.

after. After the second metal gate (green in colour) at **V 875**51 **606**63, take an immediate left uphill at the fork.

The track passes by the ruins of some roofless stone dwellings and a deserted house, followed by a small crag on the left. The track now turns mossy and boggy underfoot, and a river flows on the right in the valley below.

The terrain becomes firmer after a metal gate and the Baurearagh Valley starts to open up in front. About 200m away from here, there is a final metal gate at **V 872**04 **604**07 where the track ends. There are amazing views into the green valley as it stretches for about 2km to the cliffs that guard the eastern end of Caha. The valley is flanked by the steep side of Killane Mountain on the left, and the slopes of Coomnalack on the right. Follow the course of the Baurearagh River upstream for about 800m, keeping it to your right, to eventually cross its downflow at **V 865**86 **597**91. This is an absorbing stretch, with the beauty of the remote hillside and the pervading stillness.

The climb up to the plateau

From the stream, aim for the bottom of a spur at **V 863**71 **597**49 and ascend southwestwards up a grassy and rocky spur. After a distance of about 750m up the spur and about 240m height gain, you will arrive just below a rocky crag at **V 857**60 **592**56. Do not climb this crag, but rather outflank it to the right where the ground is grassy and scattered with purple butterwort, yellow tormentil and purple-pink ling heather.

A short distance away at **V 856**51 **591**56, the terrain on the left becomes less rocky. Here, ascend the grassy slope in order to regain the spur and head straight for its top to eventually emerge on a grassy plateau at **V 853**41 **590**81. Walk southwards, initially descending to a col, and then followed by a slight rise to the featureless summit of Caha on the broad plateau at **V 853**30 **585**59. There are views of the Caha lakes and Sugarloaf Mountain further south, in addition to Hungry Hill in the southwest.

From Caha, descend southeastwards to the col, stopping at **V 857**02 **581**59 where there are exceptional views down the Baurearagh Valley, where you walked along earlier. Next ascend a slight rise, and then swing east-northeastwards to descend to a fence at **V 861**41 **582**46. There are glimpses of Barley Lake (visited in Walk 28) to the southeast.

The panoramic view northeast from high on the Killane ridge, from nearby Beara Hills to the distant range of the Reeks, the Gap of Dunloe, Purple Mountain, Mangerton and Derrynasaggart Mountains.

The ridge of Killane

Follow the fence that runs along the Killane ridge, keeping it on the left, as the grassy ridge undulates until the fence turns a corner at **V 870**14 **592**45. Cross the fence here and continue northeastwards along the grassy ridge, over the summit of Killane Mountain followed by a slight drop, until meeting another fence at **V 875**50 **598**84. A peaty area is soon crossed and about 300m away, you will meet another fence at **V 877**51 **601**09.

Follow this line of fences to a corner at **V 883**71 **605**21 (if you wish to gain the summit of Baurearagh Mountain, you will need to cross the fence). At the corner, follow the fence that runs down the mountain towards Baurearagh Valley, keeping it to your right, as you zigzag and edge down the steep heathery slopes. The rough hillside of Coomnalack and Coomnadiha rear up menacingly to the southwest as you descend the steep slopes.

There is a patch of bracken halfway down the slope, and also a stone circle further below to the left. Keep following the fence until you reach a wall near the track below. There is a steep rock-step beyond it. Do not attempt to descend down this rock-step, but instead turn left and walk a few paces until reaching the end of another fence at **V 879**68 **610**75. Step over the fence, and very carefully pick a way down the grassy and rocky ledges to your left, later veering right to meet the track just before a metal gate.

Walk along the track then turn left at the junction to retrace steps back to the start point.

WALK 28: LAND OF A HUNDRED LAKES

One of the main attractions of this walk is its unique landscape pockmarked with lakes both large and small in a truly wild setting found nowhere else on the Beara Peninsula. Barley Lake is the largest, followed by two remote mountain lakes west of the Coomerkane Valley. The walk meets the re-routed Beara Way briefly before climbing to a rugged summit ridge for glorious views of the peninsula. It then traverses the broad plateau of Glenlough Mountain with its minefield of lakes and tarns, to cap off a memorable and challenging day.

Start/finish: Parking spaces at the cul-de-sac at the top of the road leading to Barley Lake at **V 879**97 **573**75.

Distance: 11km/6.8 miles ***Total Ascent:*** 520m/1,706ft
Walking Time: 3¾ to 4½ hours ***Maps:*** OSi Sheet 85
Walk Grade: 4

Special notes: Navigation from the summit ridge north of Toberavanaha Lough over the Glenlough Mountain plateau can be tricky, even in good weather. Navigation experience is essential and hence the walk grade of 4. The plateau is broad and relatively featureless, except for a scattering of small tarns and lakes that are testing to differentiate in the mist.

Barley Lake

Even the drive up the narrow, switchback lane to the start point east of Crossterry Mountain fills one with the feeling of expectancy as wide-ranging views northwestwards towards Killane Mountain and the valley below unfold.

From the start point, walk southwestwards for about 300m, then veer southeastwards to gradually descend to the northeastern corner of Barley Lake at **V 880**91 **568**13. The idyllic lake is nearly 800m long and 650m at its widest, tucked in a green hollow gouged out of the mountainside. The rugged col you need to get to next at its southern corner can be seen from here.

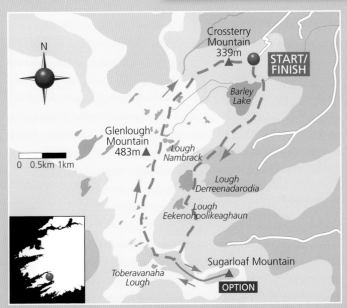

Barley Lake and Glenlough Mountain

Crossterry
Mountain
339m

START/
FINISH

Barley
Lake

Glenlough
Mountain
483m

Lough
Nambrack

Lough
Derreenadarodia

Lough
Eekenohoolikeaghaun

Sugarloaf Mountain

Toberavanaha
Lough

OPTION

N

0   0.5km 1km

*Looking southwards across Barley Lake, with Sugarloaf
Mountain poking out in the distant centre.*

Walk near the lakeshore along grassy, bracken-covered ground and aim for this col at **V 875**79 **559**48. The ground is rough and trackless (and it will be for most of the day), but once up on the col, you will be greeted with views of the valley on its other side: the whaleback profile of Sugarloaf Mountain in the far left and its ridge extending westwards.

Two lakes

From the col, descend southwestwards for a distance of about 450m along bracken-covered slopes to near where two streams meet at **V 872**40 **556**21. Scores of thick green bracken and rhododendron thickets rampage above and a stream cascades down its slopes. Cross the stream on your right. With the main stream now on your left and steep ground on your right, descend southwestwards into the grassy valley. Contour along the valley floor for about 200m, cross a tiny stream and ascend to the northeastern edge of Lough Derreenadavodia at **V 865**90 **549**62. This is truly a great spot, with the rippling blue waters of the lake, the savage backdrop of the cliffs at its western end and the brown sentinel of Sugarloaf Mountain rising beyond.

Follow the lakeshore, cross a stream and contour to its southern end with high ground on your left (look out for traces of a faint path). Once beyond the lake's southern end, ascend a gradual spur to its grassy end at **V 864**02 **543**33. From its edge, a second lake with the rather long name of Lough Eekenohoolikeaghaun (*Loch Eisceanna Chorlaí Uí Cheocháin*, 'lake at Corlaí Ó Ceocháin's esks/marshes') comes into view below. Notice a large patch of reeds also that looks a lot like a mini golf course from high up on the plateau.

The view from the col south of Barley Lake, looking towards the slopes of Sugarloaf Mountain on the left and its ridge extending westwards. The waters of Lough Derreenadavodia and Lough Eekenohoolikeaghaun can just be seen in the mid-ground.

The nameless summit

Next, ascend the trackless ground southeastwards, then later veer southwestwards to the obvious spur above.

In the height of summer the ground is sprinkled liberally with colours of flora and fauna: yellow tormentil, pale-pink heath-spotted orchid, blue-violet butterwort, white bog-cotton, red-purple bell heather and with damselflies – blue tail, common blue damselflies and large red ones – gracing the air.

Once on the spur, you will reach yellow-white wooden signposts marking a section of the Beara Way at **V 864**30 **534**76. Follow the waymarkers to a col at **V 862**30 **532**63 just below a summit on your right. Here, leave the Beara Way and strike for the summit above you. A small pile of rocks marks this nameless summit on the OSi map, due west of Sugarloaf Mountain, at **V 860**67 **532**86.

Sugarloaf Mountain (574m/1,883ft) extension: It is possible to ascend Sugarloaf Mountain from the col before the nameless summit. From the col, ascend a slight rise southeastwards, then descend to another col above Kealagowlane, before finally pulling up to the summit of Sugarloaf Mountain, marked by its chalk-white trig point at **V 873**76 **529**51. For this extension, add 2.5km/1.6 miles to the distance, 200m/656ft to the total ascent, and 1 to 1¼ hours to the total walking time. The summit provides good views of Bantry Bay and Sheep's Head to the south and also Coomerkane Valley and the wooded slopes of Derrynafulla to the north.

Lough Eekenohoolikeaghaun and Lough Derreenadavodia sitting in the wild valley west of Coomerkane, with the Caha Mountains beyond, as seen from the nameless summit at **V 860**67 **532**86.

Lakeland

From the nameless summit, head westwards, negotiating some easy rock slabs, then descend into a rugged hollow at **V 857**81 **534**46. Scramble up a rock step, and then contour along some easy-angled rock slabs, keeping high ground on your left and the valley on your right, gradually swinging northwestwards. The ground drops slightly, and the terrain is featureless. You will eventually reach a small tarn at **V 855**89 **537**91, and even on a clear day you may need to take a bearing. From here, head roughly northwards over featureless terrain. You may pass some tarns along the way, depending on the course you take. A good intermediate point to assess your location is a tarn at **V 857**70 **548**78, and a bearing may also be required to arrive.

One location you should go to is the top of a grassy knoll overlooking some lakes, marked as Lough Nambrack on the OSi map at **V 859**41 **554**63. This is an amazing spot – as remote and wild as it gets at close quarters, and with wide-ranging views of Knockboy (706m/2,316ft) and the Shehy Mountains beyond.

From here, walk for just over 1km on undulating ground, for a large extent between a string of lakes, and then followed by a gradual descent to the northern corner of a lake – the final one you will meet on the plateau, at **V 863**16 **565**70.

Next, head northeastwards along the spur for about 550m to **V 867**11 **569**71. Here descend the grassy slopes to your right, then contour along its sides, with the spur above you on your left, to reach a broad grassy gap. A gradual ascent to point 339m follows, reaching a fence corner at **V 873**37 **572**22. Now simply follow the fence as it leads back to the start point.

Looking northeastwards across Lough Nambrack and its lakes from a grassy knoll on the plateau of Glenlough Mountain.

Bibliography

Bardwell, Sandra, Fairbairn, Helen and McCormack, Gareth, *Walking in Ireland* (Lonely Planet Publications, 2003).

Dunne, John, *Irish Lake Marvels: Mysteries, Legends and Lore* (Liberties Press, 2009).

Flanagan, Deirdre and Flanagan, Laurence, *Irish Place Names* (Gill & Macmillan, 1994).

Gray, Peter, *The Irish Famine* (H. N. Abrams, 1995).

Hendroff, Adrian, *From High Places: A Journey Through Ireland's Great Mountains* (The History Press Ireland, 2010).

Hill, Pete, Johnston, Stuart, *The Mountain Skills Training Handbook* (David & Charles, 2nd edition, 2009).

Holland, Charles H. and Sanders, Ian S., *The Geology of Ireland* (Dunedin Academic Press, 2nd revised edition, 2009).

Langmuir, Eric, *Mountaincraft and Leadership* (Sportscotland and the MLTB, 3rd edition, 1995).

Long, Steve, MTT staff, *Hillwalking: The Official Handbook of the Mountain Leader and Walking Group Leader Schemes* (Mountain Leader Training UK, 2003).

Lynam, Joss, *Best Irish Walks* (Gill & Macmillan, 2001).

MacDonogh, Steve, *The Dingle Peninsula: History, Folklore, Archaeology* (Brandon Press, 1993).

MacNeill, Maire, *The Festival of Lughnasa: A Study of the Survival of the Celtic Festival of the Beginning of Harvest* (Folklore of Ireland Council, 2008)

Massey, Eithne, *Legendary Ireland: Myths and Legends of Ireland* (O'Brien Press, 2005).

Pilcher, Jon. R., Hall, Valerie, *Flora Hibernica: The Wild Flowers, Plants and Trees of Ireland* (The Collins Press, 2004).

Raymo, Chet, *Climbing Brandon: Science and Faith on Ireland's Holy Mountain* (Walker & Company, 2004).

Ryan, Jim, *Carrauntoohil & MacGillycuddy's Reeks: A Walking Guide to Ireland's Highest Mountains* (The Collins Press, 2006).

Ryan, Jim, 'The toothless Stumpa in Hag's Glen', *Irish Mountain Log* No. 82 (Summer 2007).

Severin, Tim, *The Brendan Voyage* (Abacus, 1996).

Smith, Charles, *The Antient and Present State of the County of Kerry* (1756).

Smith, Michael, *An Unsung Hero: Tom Crean – Antarctic Survivor* (The Collins Press, 2000).

Somers, Dermot, *Endurance: Heroic Journeys in Ireland* (O'Brien Press, 2005).

Sterry, Paul and Mooney, Derek, *Collins Complete Guide to Irish Wildlife* (Collins, 2010).

Tempan, Paul, 'Some Notes on the Names of Six Kerry Mountains', *Journal of the Kerry Archaeological and Historical Society*, Series 2, Vol. 5 (2005), pp. 5–19.

Thomas, Clive, *GPS for Walkers: An Introduction to GPS and Digital Maps* (Jarrold Publishing, 2006).

Weld, Isaac, *Illustrations of the Scenery of Killarney and the Surrounding Country* (Longman Hurst etc., 1812).

Williams, R. A., *The Berehaven Copper Mines: Allihies, Co. Cork, S.W. Ireland* (Northern Mine Research Society, 1991).